HARRY THE POLIS
NUTHIN' LIKE THE TRUTH

· · ·

HARRY MORRIS

First published 2006
by Black & White Publishing Ltd
99 Giles Street, Edinburgh, EH6 6BZ

ISBN 13: 978 1 84502 120 7
ISBN 10: 1 84502 120 7

Typeset by RefineCatch Ltd, Bungay, Suffolk
Printed by Nørhaven Paperback A/S

• • •

In memory of Pauline Tourlamain

• • •

Acknowledgements

· · ·

My sincere gratitude to all the loved ones, friends, family and acquaintances who stood by me and helped me along the long arduous road of expressing my love of the Glesca patter and my literary madness, which I shared with my colleagues and now with you in these pages.

You know who you are!

I want to express my love and appreciation to Marion for helping me realise my dream to forge a lifetime of stories and anecdotes into the writing of this book.

I'm also extremely grateful for the professional help and guidance I have been given by various newspapers and radio stations to accomplish my goal.

Thanks to John Downie and Bob Shields, who gave me valuable advice prior to the publication of the Harry the Polis books and have now become good friends.

Special thanks to my friend Gordon Tourlamain.

Yours Aye, Harry Morris.

Slàinte!

'Ye just cannae beat Glesca for the real life patter.'

Passive Smokers

· · ·

Deciding to try and do something about my being over-weight and unfit since retiring from the police, I enrolled with the local fitness club.

Having been unable to exercise properly for several years owing to an injury, I had no sports equipment left and went shopping for a 'look at me' tracksuit and training shoes.

I entered a large sporting superstore and made my way to the shoe department, on the first leg to at least looking the part.

A male customer was in conversation with the shop assistant.

'I'm no' kidding ye, but after forty five minutes he was absolutely knackered. He was even struggling to draw a breath.'

'Aye, but is he no' a smoker?' asked the assistant.

'He is,' the man replied. 'But it shouldn't affect his breathing as bad as that! I should know, 'cause I smoke as well and I'm all right.'

There was a short pause before the assistant informed him, 'Did I tell ye my faither's in hospital?'

'Is he? Whit's wrang this time?' asked the customer.

'Lung cancer. The family cannae believe it, 'cause he stoaped the smoking three weeks ago and had stuck more patches on his arm than there is on a home-made quilt!'

'That's unbelievable!' responded the sympathetic customer.

'Ah know,' replied the assistant. 'Jist when he gave it up tae! My Maw's gonnae sue the Labour Club where my faither drinks – she's blaming it on passive smoking!'

Show Me Yer Jean Brodie

• • •

A police officer was awaiting his wife coming out of the bath so that he could go into the bathroom and perform the three S's: a shave, a shower and a sh-sh-shampoo!

His wife came into the lounge with a towel wrapped turban-style around her damp hair and wearing a rather elegant and comfortable-looking dressing gown, whilst her husband went upstairs to the bathroom.

A few minutes passed, then there was a knock on the front door and the wife answered it.

Standing on the doorstep was David Paisley, a former police colleague of her husband's.

'Hi, Helen. Is Robert in?' he asked her.

'He is,' she replied. 'But he's just gone upstairs for a shower.'

'Is that right?' he replied, his body language changing. He then said, 'I bet you look absolutely gorgeous under that dressing gown.'

Helen was flattered but also very embarrassed at David's personal comments and attention.

'I'll tell you what, Helen – I'll give you a hundred pounds if you let me see yer tits!' he told her.

'What?! What the hell do you think I am, David Paisley?!' she replied in disgust.

'Woah, woah! Calm down, Helen darling. It's not a big deal! I'm only asking for a wee look at yer diddies! Even just the one – just slip yer dressing gown to one side so I can have a wee butcher's hook at them and I'll give ye a hundred quid!' he pleaded.

Helen pondered for a moment while thinking over his offer ('£100 just to see one of my breasts . . .?').

'OK!' she said. 'But just the one and nae groping me.'

At that she put her head to the side, making sure her husband was still in the bathroom. Satisfied that he was, she pulled her dressing gown to one side, exposing her bare left breast.

As she covered herself up again, David handed her over the £100 in cash.

Helen quickly took the money and placed it in her dressing-gown pocket.

'Helen! Helen, that was amazing! Better than I could ever have imagined. Please don't be embarrassed – you have a beautiful body for your age! In fact, I'll tell you what – you've excited me and turned me on that much . . . I'll give you another hundred pounds if you give me a swatch downstairs.'

Helen was shocked and blushed at this new request.

'C'mon, Helen, a hundred pounds just to pull yer dressing gown to one side and gie me a wee peek at yer beaver!' he offered her.

Again she thought for a moment before tilting her head to one side to listen out for her husband.

Convinced he was still in the shower, she said, 'Aw right, but ye better no' try and touch me, ya clatty bastert, or I'll kick ye in the balls!'

She then pulled her dressing gown up and to the side, exposing her downstairs private parts.

As she again covered up, she said, 'Quick! Give me my money.'

David held up his side of the bargain and, having paid her the money, said, 'I'll tell ye what, Helen, if I said you had a beautiful body, would you hold it against me? I've got another hundred pounds here and it's all yours if ye open up yer dressing gown and let me gie ye a squeeze and a wee cuddle.'

Helen responded immediately, 'Away you an' bile yer heid, ya bloody sick pervert! Coming to my front door and asking me tae dae aw that! Whit dae ye take me for?' She continued, 'And another thing – whit if some bugger was tae see us?'

'Aw! C'mon, Helen, nae bugger can see us. Just a wee cuddle, that's all. I've always fancied you! What harm can it do?' he reasoned with her. 'C'mon, Helen!' At that, David began to sing to her, 'If I said you had a beautiful body would you hold it against me?'

Quick as a flash, Helen responded, 'A hundred pounds?'

'My hand tae God, a hundred quid, in yer hand like before!' replied David sincerely.

Helen again thought for a moment, pondering David's latest proposition, while listening out for her husband getting out of the shower.

Her mind made up, she said, 'Right!' Putting her hand out to relieve David of his third £100, she placed it into her pocket before loosening her dressing-gown belt and revealing her shapely mature naked body.

At that moment, David put his hands around the inside of her dressing gown and gave her a tight squeeze and a cuddle.

Suddenly she could hear her husband Robert getting out of the shower.

'Right! Enough! Enough!' she said. 'Now bugger off.'

Pushing David away, she closed her front door over.

She stood for a moment, composing herself as she reflected on her easy earnings, before re-entering the lounge, where Robert was about to sit down in his armchair in front of the television.

'Was that the front door I heard?' he asked.

'The front door? No!' replied Helen. 'Why, are you expecting someone?'

To which Robert replied, 'Aye! That wee sleekit bastard David Paisley! He owes me three hundred quid and promised me faithfully he would call at the house tonight and hand it over!!'

Check the Menu

• • •

On a night out to a local Chinese restaurant, I was sitting at my table perusing the menu when my attention was drawn to a waiter standing near by, blatantly scratching his bum.

'Excuse me!' I said. 'But do you have an itchy arse?'

To which he responded by walking over to me and saying, in all sincerity, 'If it's not on de menu, I will ash de chef if we do it!'

Now, you have to wonder if that'll be with fried rice or noodles?

Speed Camera Excuses

. . .

'I was on my way to the airport to uplift my husband and was in the flight path and I'm positive the speed camera was triggered off by his incoming aeroplane overhead and certainly not by my car!'

Mushroom Joke

. . .

There was a detective sergeant I worked with who was too nice and polite to be a cop.

During a tea break in the office, I was telling him a joke which went like this.

'Did you hear about the wee mushroom who went out drinking and dancing every night?' I paused for a moment before continuing, 'He was a "fun-gi" to be with!'

Alan laughed and said, 'That was a good one, Harry. I must remember it!'

Later the same day, I entered the office and Alan was with the detective inspector and a few other CID officers.

'Wait till I tell you this joke!' he said very enthusiastically.

With the complete attention of all present, he said, 'What do you call a wee mushroom who goes out dancing and drinking every night with all his friends?'

'I don't know,' said one of the officers.

Whereby Alan replied, 'A "fun-fellow" to be with!'

I swear he got a bigger laugh than I did, and I told the joke right!

Real Answers from Police Scotland Exams

. . .

These are some genuine answers submitted by students during the Police Scotland Exams 2004.

'Malicious mischief is a crime at common law and is when someone steals flowers and tramples on grass.'
'A house is any place that has plumbing fitted.'
'Indecent assault – touching yourself in a sexual manner.'

Apparently just about every police officer sitting the exams on the day admitted being guilty of number 3.

Kids, You've Got To Love Them

. . .

A colleague of mine received appreciation letters from a local primary school, thanking him for showing them around the police station during their recent visit.

However, one letter stated, 'Thank you for letting me visit your police station. Until I met you, I didn't know what a criminal really looked like up close'!

I do hope my colleague didn't confuse the child!

Kids' Stuff

...

At one point during my service on the police motorcycles, I was assigned, with my colleague Davy Hall, to perform a regular visit to secondary schools in the Strathclyde area and talk to them about the specific job we were performing as police motorcyclists.

This would also entail us explaining all the parts of our motorcycles, including make, model, engine size, speed, etc.

After this talk, we would then welcome questions from our young audience.

One day, whilst at a school in Kingspark, Glasgow, we were answering the usual questions after our lecture.

A young girl was trying to ask a question but every time she began to speak, a boy in her class would interrupt and speak over her.

Each time the boy did this, Davy would ask him to wait his turn until he had heard what the young girl had to ask.

The boy, however, ignored Davy's advice and continued to speak over her.

Eventually Davy had endured enough of his rude interruptions and told him so, in no uncertain terms.

The boy stared at Davy for a moment then uttered, 'Fuck off!'

Unable to restrain himself, Davy grabbed hold of the boy's collar and almost pulled him over the motorcycle.

On seeing this, I intervened and took the boy away and reported his involvement to the head teacher.

The head teacher informed us that he would be dealt

with and we would receive thank you letters from all the pupils who attended our crime prevention/community involvement talk, coupled with a special letter of apology from the rude boy for his abuse towards Davy.

About a week later, as promised, we received a large mail bag of letters.

Included was the apology from the rude boy, which read as follows:

> *Dear Constable Hall,*
> *I would like to say I am very sorry for being so rude towards you during your visit to our school, it was very informative.*
> *Thomas Wilson*

However, at the bottom left corner of the letter were the words,

> *PS. Ya big arse.*

It appears that after checking what the students had written, the head teacher returned the letters to each pupil to place them into a sealed envelope addressed to us.

Thus Thomas had taken the opportunity of adding his postscript while unsupervised.

Kids – don't you just love them?

The Patient's 'Armless'

* * *

Early one morning, prior to going off duty after a long and arduous twelve-hour shift, Barry Potts (nicknamed 'Bam') and I, along with the rest of our colleagues, were gathered in the police garage when a call came over the radio regarding a train crash at Polmadie in Glasgow.

Everyone present jumped back into their squad cars and headed for the location to give assistance.

On our arrival, there were sirens wailing and klaxons blaring as all the emergency units of police, fire and ambulance descended upon the area as one.

A quick assessment of the devastation revealed the traction engine and several of the carriages had been derailed and overturned, with the train driver trapped under the overturned traction engine.

The fire service personnel worked away in an effort to free the driver.

Using portable hydraulic jacks, they made several attempts to lift the engine off his trapped arm, but to no avail.

Eventually, the Royal Infirmary surgical squad, or as some of the services cruelly dubbed them, the Butchers' Department, arrived to take over the situation.

With the driver in shock, coupled with an excessive amount of blood loss, the decision was taken by the senior member of the Butchers' Squad to amputate the driver's trapped arm in order to free him and have him conveyed by ambulance and police escort to the nearest hospital.

For our part, Bam and I were detailed to provide

the high-speed police escort through the busy Glasgow streets.

The Royal's surgical squad crawled under the engine and performed the amputation, thereby freeing the driver.

We then carried out the next part of the emergency procedure, arriving at our destination in practically no time at all.

As we were about to drive off, a young nurse came running out of the entrance, frantically waving her arms at us to attract our attention.

We immediately pulled up and stopped as she ran over to us.

'His arm!' she screamed. 'Where is his arm?'

Bam and I looked at each other, slightly puzzled.

'We assumed it was in the ambulance alongside him!' I replied.

'Well, it's not and the surgeon requires it here immediately in order to try and save it. So will you go back and get it?' she asked.

In layman's terms, the emergency team and their patient were completely 'armless'!

As quick as we had arrived at the hospital, we returned to the scene of the train crash to collect our missing arm.

Having radioed ahead about our dilemma, a rail worker was waiting for us and he came running over to our car with the arm wrapped in a towel.

'Excuse me, sir, but wid ye just like tae check the fingers on this arm and confirm there are two gold rings and a tattoo of a Highland bagpiper?'

He then opened the towel to expose the train driver's full arm, which was saturated with his blood.

I couldn't believe what I had just heard, so I asked him, 'What did you just say there?'

He repeated, 'I want you to check out his hand, because I need a signature from you that I gave you an arm with two gold rings and a tattoo on it. It's just tae keep me right wi' my gaffers in case they had to go missing!' he explained.

Bam looked at him and said, 'Are you fuckin' stupid? Who the fuck is going tae steal an amputated arm with a tattoo and two rings on it, ya bammy bastard?'

'Well, ye never know,' he replied in all seriousness. 'I'm just covering my back and keeping mysel' right.'

'Well, I'm not signing anything,' said Bam rather indignantly.

'Fine!' said the rail worker. 'Then I'm not giving you his fuckin' arm.'

At this point, I had to intervene to calm things down.

'Woah there, mate!' I said. 'Put that arm in the back seat of the police car and don't be so stupid!'

'No way, not without a signature in my book!' he replied.

Bam interrupted, 'How about I give ye a signature wi' my police baton across yer stupid heid, ya thick bastard?'

'Right, that's it. I'm going tae see my gaffer about you swearing and threatening me.' At that, he walked away.

I quickly got out of the police car.

'Wait a minute, mate. Let's get a reality check here. There's a colleague of yours lying in the operating theatre of the hospital down the road, with a team of surgeons round him, waiting on us arriving back with an arm, in order to try and sew it back on. Now unless you've got something better to do with his arm, like maybe a triple-arm-wrestling competition, I suggest ye give it to me and let me get on with my job of "hand" delivering it!'

He thought for a moment before handing me the arm.

As I took possession of it, he said, 'Mind and check the rings and tattoo are there,' before adding, 'I just hope this left arm is the right one.'

There was no answer to that last remark, apart from the fact he had just confirmed to both of us he was definitely a thick bastard!

As I placed the arm on the back seat, he shouted over, 'I hope it doesn't fall off that seat!'

To which I responded, 'Don't be silly – it's holding on to the door handle.'

'Armed' with our important despatch, we delivered it safely to its destination, with tattoo and rings still intact, and the surgeons were able to perform a successful operation to reattach it.

Although Bam reckons they sewed his arm on back to front and he now gives you the thumbs up and thumbs down at the same time!

You're a sick man, Pottsy!

The Polis Interpreter

· · ·

A Chinese man was apprehended and conveyed to the police station, suspected of theft and credit card fraud.

During interview, the man deliberately gave the impression to the arresting officers that he could not speak or understand any English.

The officers were convinced their suspect was deliberately delaying proceedings and could understand and speak English fluently.

However, the duty inspector intervened and informed the arresting officers that they must go by the book and contact an interpreter for their Chinese prisoner, to inform him of his legal rights before they could proceed any further.

One of the cops went through to the front office to call the force control room, to try and find a Chinese interpreter available to attend.

Whilst he was doing this, Gerry Docherty, a uniformed cop, approached him and asked, 'Who jailed wee Sammy Wang?'

'I did!' replied the young cop. 'But the bugger doesn't speak a word of English so the inspector wants me to get an interpreter from Pitt Street for him.'

'Don't bother phoning Pitt Street,' said Gerry. 'I know Sammy well – I'll interpret for you!'

'Oh, brilliant, Gerry. You speak Chinese?' asked the cop.

'Not really,' replied Gerry. 'But I eat a lot of Chinese grub so I think that qualifies me to be able to speak Sammy's language!'

Gerry walked along the corridor and entered the interview room where Sammy was sitting.

On seeing Gerry enter the room, Sammy sat upright in his seat, whereby Gerry promptly slapped him across the head.

'So all of a sudden you don't speak English, Sammy?' asked Gerry. 'Well, let's try and help you with some useful tips.'

At that he gave Sammy an almighty thump, knocking him clear off his chair, and as he was preparing to do so again, Sammy screamed out, 'All wight! All wight! I speak the fuckin' Engwish! No need to take it so sewiously!'

Gerry turned to the arresting cops and said, 'There ye go, boys. He just needed a wee reminder that he has a perfect understanding of the English language.' He then imitated Sammy: 'Would you wike flied lice wiff your charge?'

As Gerry left the interview room, he was met in the corridor by the duty inspector.

'What's all the commotion?' he asked.

'Nothing to concern you, Inspector. I was just giving Sammy a crash course in English in order to save time and the added expense of an interpreter!'

This was achieved not only by Gerry's local knowledge and understanding of the language, but more importantly, knowing how to interpret and administer it properly.

Nothing to do with the police manual or political correctness, much to the annoyance of the duty inspector.

However, Gerry added that it helps considerably if you eat regularly in the Chinese restaurant where Sammy works as a waiter and therefore know him personally!!

Uncle Tommy

. . .

My uncle Tommy was a Royal Mail postman who, after many years of climbing up tenement stairs to deliver the mail, decided he would go for a job as a collecting van driver.

Not in possession of a full driving licence, he set about getting lessons in order to redress this situation and sit his driving test.

After many hours of costly lessons came the big day for his driving test.

Off he went with 'good luck' messages from all his family ringing in his ears.

However, en route to the test centre his nerves got the better of him so, in order to get back on course and settle himself down, Uncle Tommy decided to stop off at his local public house where he quickly downed two large whiskies.

Feeling slightly more confident and relaxed, Uncle Tommy arrived at the test centre a short time later.

As he sat in the waiting room, he eventually got the call, 'Thomas Docherty!'

'That's me, pal!' Tommy replied to the examiner standing before him with a pen and clipboard in hand.

As the examiner greeted him, a strong waft of stale Scotch whisky tested his senses.

'Excuse me, Mr Docherty, but have you been drinking?' asked the examiner.

Uncle Tommy replied, 'Drinking? In the plural, naw! Drink? In the singular, yes! As you can see for yersel', son,

I've only had the wan, purely for medicinal purposes, you understand, just to calm my nerves. You know what Ah mean, pal? It can be bloody nerve-wracking out on they busy roads! Mind you, I don't need to tell *you* that. You've probably had a few haufs yersel' afore ye started yer work!'

'Indeed I did not! And you can't have a drink either and expect to come along here today and sit a driving test!' said the irate examiner.

'And why not?' asked Uncle Tommy in all sincerity. 'The boys in my mail depot told me you are allowed up to two drinks at least!'

The examiner gave him a stern look before cancelling his test and walking off in total disgust and disbelief.

Several years later, after he had emigrated to Australia, I learned that Uncle Tommy had finally passed his driving test, which I found hard to believe, but then again, Foster's Driving Test Centre in Castlemaine don't really give a XXXX!

Signs
• • •

I passed a tattoo parlour the other day and it was advertising that they also performed body piercing, but there was another sign which confused me that read, 'Ears pierced while you wait'!

How would they do it if you don't want to wait?

Bethnal Green Escort

· · ·

My partner, big Joe, and I were performing surveillance on premises when we received a call to return to the station as we were required for a prisoner escort.

'Go home, get changed and return as quickly as possible!' said the chief inspector. 'I want you both to catch the four o'clock train from Glasgow Central to Euston Station, London, and collect a prisoner on warrant, being held at Bethnal Green police station. You'll return with him on the following morning train.'

Off we went, returning in no time at all, to be whisked off to the station via the off-licence for a much-needed carry-out for the long train journey.

'What's in the wee bag?' big Joe asked me.

'I'll tell you later, big man! It's on a need to know basis. It doesn't affect you right now though!' I replied.

Once the train had left the station, I was aware that big Joe was not in possession of an overnight bag, like mine, with toiletries or a change of shirt. I made no mention of it at the time, but I knew from experience what was ahead for him.

After several hours' drinking on the train, we had exhausted our carry-out and needed to visit the buffet bar for some much-needed reinforcements, because we were both greedy bastards.

Before our arrival at Euston Station and prior to the bar closing, big Joe ordered two extra bottles of Grolsch lager for his morning-after, 'hair of the dog' Scottish remedy for hangovers, concealing them in his jacket inside breast pocket.

I visited the toilet to wash my face and smarten myself up for our meeting with the officers who would be at the station to greet us.

On our arrival, we were met by our transport and whisked off to Bethnal Green police station to check in on our prisoner and submit the warrant documentation required in order to transfer him into our custody and bring him back to Scotland.

After the pleasantries, I made arrangements for us to collect our prisoner the following morning.

I then asked our driver if he could drive us to a public house for a few beers before we went to our overnight accommodation.

Whilst in the process of taking us somewhere, I heard the driver answering a call and saying, 'I have the detective inspector and the detective sergeant in the car heading for . . .' and he gave our location. Then, 'Affirmative – Inspector Cohen will rendezvous with him there!'

The driver informed us that the shift inspector and sergeant wished to meet with us and take us for something to eat and drink.

Good one, I thought – promotion and a bevvy. That will do for me!

We met up with our new escorts who drove us to a quiet little Greek kebab shop.

As we entered the front door, we were shown to our table at the rear of the shop, out of public view.

We sat down and the inspector introduced us to our host as very important detectives from Glasgow.

'We bring our guests here all the time,' he said before

ordering up four large brandies and four special Greek kebabs.

Within a short time, more brandy arrived, followed by our meal.

As we talked about the usual police stuff, I was aware that the inspector and sergeant had their food served to them in box cartons, while our meals were on plates.

The inspector explained, 'Well, we're going to leave you to enjoy your meal. Duty calls and all that. I don't have to tell you what it's like!' They both stood up and said, 'We hope you enjoy the rest of your night!'

As they left the shop, big Joe ordered up another two large brandies while I concentrated on eating my scrumptiously delicious kebab.

'Do me a Rodney Laver and eat up a bit faster, big man!' I said.

'Why?' asked Joe, sitting back in his chair with brandy in hand, enjoying the ambience of our back-shop surroundings.

'Because that pair of fly bastards left without putting their hands in their pockets to pay for this lot and I'm certainly not going to pay the bill for them! So gub it down faster while I think of something!' I replied anxiously.

Joe paused for a moment, then it sunk in. 'Pair of bastards – they're trying to hump us for a free drink and a free meal?'

'Exactly!' I replied. 'Now just say nothing and leave me to do the talking!'

I ordered up a bottle of Keo brandy to take away in a carry-out and then picked up a card for the kebab shop and asked to use the telephone (no mobile phones in those days). I then contacted our escort driver and gave him the address where he should pick us up.

Then, closely followed by big Joe, who was carrying the newly acquired bottle of brandy, I walked out to the front of the shop and stopped at the serving counter, before presenting my hand and shaking the owner's.

'What a meal, Stelios. It was absolutely brilliant. Inspector Cohen knew exactly what he was doing when he brought us in here. Anyway, I've just spoken with Inspector Cohen on the phone and he said to let you know he doesn't want us paying anything towards the meal and that he will return to square you up for the entire bill later. So let me just say thanks again for a really good night!'

'He is paying bill?' asked Stelios, slightly bemused. 'But he say *you* will pay!'

'Well,' I said, continuing with my bluff, 'he's obviously changed his mind, Stelios, and has insisted on paying for it. He's got loadsa money and it was his treat, so he wants to pay it all! That's why he told us to order up a bottle of Keo brandy. He's joining us afterwards for a drink!' I finished, very convincingly.

Turning to big Joe, I whispered out of the corner of my mouth, 'Quick, there's our lift outside. Shake his hand and let's GTF.'

We then left the shop, got in our car and were driven off.

'Good food in there, but it's a bit expensive,' said our driver.

'It's certainly is,' I replied, with a wry smile.

'Where to now, sir?' he asked.

'Could you take us to a good English-style pub where we can get a decent pint of best bitter?' I said.

'There's not too many still open at this time of night, but I'll see what I can do for you.'

He then drove us to an area where he got out of the car and told us to wait while he checked it out for us.

He then walked up a narrow lane, returning moments later.

'Right, it's closed, but I've told him who you are and he's willing to let you in for a few beers!' explained our driver. 'Now, walk up the lane until you see a red door on your left and give it a good bang. The owner's name is Ranjid – he'll let you in the back and when you're ready to be picked up again, get him to call me on this number.'

He handed me his calling card.

We followed the driver's instructions to a T and were invited in by a young Asian guy name Hamed.

As we walked through to the lounge area – shockeroony!

It was packed full of our Asian brothers. There must have been about twenty-five or thirty of them inside, and guess who they were all staring at? You've guessed it!

The two 'pale face' dudes who have just gatecrashed their local hostelry.

Fortunately they couldn't understand us and most of them assumed we were probably the latest consignment of refugees to arrive in London. Especially with me carrying my wee bag!

'By the way, what is in the wee bag?' asked Joe again.

'I'll tell ye later!' I replied. 'Now order up the "Don Revie"!'

With subtlety and the aid of sign language, big Joe ordered up our drinks. 'Ho, Rancid! Give us a couple o' pints of yer "breast butter", if you would.'

I quickly intervened, 'Sorry, Ranjid! He means two pints of your best bitter, please!'

With all eyes on us, big Joe said, 'Let's show these boys how it's done!' He then uttered, 'Cheers for the beers and here's tae the queers – bottoms up!'

He then gulped down half of his pint, only stopping to breathe, fart and burp, all at the same time I might add. Talented or what?

Then all hell broke loose!

'Fuckin' hell, Rancid! I think a cat's pished doon yer beer pipes!' big Joe blurted out, while dribbling from his mouth.

'It's Ranjid!' I corrected him.

'You're telling *me* it's ranjid!' replied big Joe. 'I've just fuckin' swallowed hauf o' it.' He then held his pint towards me and said, 'Fuckin' taste that pish yersel'. It's bowfin, and you know me, Harry, I'll drink my beer through a wean's shitty nappy!'

'What do you want me to do about it?' I asked him.

'Fuckin' tell him. You're the DI efter all. I'm only the DS.'

Undeterred, he then took another gulp from his pint glass, just to confirm it was rancid.

'Madras! I can fuckin' taste curry as well as pish!' he cried, spilling some of the liquid over his shirt and trousers.

'Look at that! It's even taking the colour oot my bastarding new shirt! Ho, Hamheid! Check this out.'

'Right, Joe, it's Hamed, so enough! Drink up and let's

GTF,' I said, sensing an uncomfortable atmosphere amongst our new friends, with Joe slagging off their best amber liquid.

'Drink up?' Joe replied in disgust. 'Are ye fuckin' mad? I'd rather drink my ain urine. Anyways, I'm putting my name up on the board – I want tae play a game o' pool wi' Hamheid and some of his ethnic soul brothers.'

I whispered in his ear, 'If you don't keep yer voice down a bit, we just might end up floating upside down in a pool, courtesy of Hamed and his soul brothers. Now follow me and let's go. Now!'

I turned to Ranjid and asked him to call the number on the card while Joe paid for our beers, which were extortionately overpriced.

'Excuse me, Rancid! But did I order drinks for everybody at the bar? 'Cause I think you've fuckin' jist charged me for them,' remarked big Joe.

'Forget it!' I told Joe. 'Let's just get out of here.'

'Forget it?' replied an irate Joe. 'Well, why don't I drop my trousers and let him park his rickshaw between the cheeks o' my arse as well?'

'Rickshaws are Chinese, ya big diddy!' I said, correcting him.

'Well, chapatti, then!' he responded.

At that, Ranjid enquired in a snide manner, 'So, boys, did you enjoy your beers, then?'

'Yeah!' I said. 'Very mucky indeed with a distinct taste of keegh to add a bit of body. In fact, it was full of it – obviously a blend of your own special brew. I presume it's popular!'

He stared at me with a vacant look on his face, totally oblivious to what I was talking about.

As I shook his hand, I said, 'Well, thanks for that, Ranjid, and as we say in Scotland, you've been an absolute tadger of a host and a real douche bag, so you and Hamed have a nice day!'

We then left by the back door and, fortunately for us, only our driver was waiting outside to meet us at the entrance to the lane.

I decided we would head for our overnight accommodation and enjoy our bottle of brandy, acquired at the expense of Inspector Cohen and his sidekick sergeant.

Next morning I rose early and, after I had showered and shaved, I went to big Joe's room and found his door unlocked, so I entered.

With the windows closed all night, the room smelt worse than Ranjid's best bitter.

Big Joe had also visited his toilet during the night and forgot to flush the pan.

Sitting on his dressing table were his two bottles of Grolsch for his hangover cure.

I quickly removed the tops and poured the contents down the sink. I then filled them with lukewarm tap water before replacing them.

All the while I was in his room, Joe slept like a baby, interrupting his snoring with the occasional loud fart!

His suit was lying on the floor where he had discarded it the previous night and he was still wearing his shirt in bed.

I went back to my room to get dressed and put on my clean shirt.

With my teeth brushed and my tie straight, I put my soiled shirt and toiletries back in my overnight bag and knocked loudly on big Joe's door before opening it.

'Rise and shine, big man, or you're going to be late for your breakfast!'

'What time is it?' he enquired in his drowsy hungover state.

'It's now eight o'clock and we are getting picked up at nine, so you'd better get yer arse into gear and I'll meet you downstairs in the restaurant.'

'Right! Right, I'm coming!' he shouted back.

Having enjoyed my cooked English breakfast, I was relaxing with a cup of coffee, reading the morning newspaper, when an apparition appeared before me. It was big Joe, standing there in his soiled shirt and crushed suit, with his hair tousled and sticking up.

He was totally minging and dressed like a burst bin bag!

He then said with deep sincerity, 'I hope we get the same train back up the road.'

'How come?' I asked.

''Cause that wee bastard Dai serving at the buffet bar sold me two bottles o' fuckin' warm water, the wee Welsh twat!'

'You're kidding?!' I said, trying to appear surprised.

'Naw, I am no' kidding!' he replied. 'The wee bastard! I'll fuckin' "Dai" him.' He then looked around the breakfast tables. 'Anything for drinking here? I'm choking for a swally. I'd even drink a pint o' Rancid's stale pish!'

'Get yourself a glass of milk!' I said condescendingly.

As he stood there looking at me, he let his eyes focus upon the bag beside me, then the penny dropped.

'Overnight bag with a clean shirt, toothbrush and a razor?' he enquired dejectedly.

I nodded my head and grinned like a Cheshire cat.

'I suppose I look like a bag o' shit, right?' he asked.

'Definitely!' I replied.

'I'm gonnae look more like your prisoner than *he* is!' he remarked.

I nodded again, still grinning.

To which he responded rather disconsolately by looking me straight in the face and saying, '*Bastard*! Sorry – *DI Bastard*!'

Bonfire Night

. . .

At a recent visit to Glasgow Green on Guy Fawkes Night to watch the excellent bonfire and firework display, I was reminded of a story that 'Tank', my favourite scrap metal dealer from Bridgeton, told me.

It was about a woman that lived in the Bridgeton area many years ago, when he was a young boy, and she was nicknamed by everyone who knew her as 'Bonnie'!

Apparently she was called that because every 'Guy' within a three-mile radius had been on top of her!

Dial a Letter

· · ·

From The Adventures of Harry the Polis

(Harry is in with the superintendent, who is making Harry aware of the new sexual harassment laws in the force.)

SUPT: Harry! I would like you to watch what you say to these female station assistants. They'll twist your every word.

HARRY: Don't worry about me, boss. I won't give them any cause for complaint.

SUPT: You know what they're like – they'll look for double meanings, so be diligent at all times, Harry.

HARRY: I won't slip up, boss!

(Harry returns to the front office and is sitting reading his newspaper when the office door opens and in walks the female station assistant.)

STATION ASSITANT: Excuse me, Harry, but can I use your dictaphone?

(Quick as a flash . . .)

HARRY: *Not on yer life, darling!* You'll just use your finger like everybody else!

Plastic Surgery

. . .

Georgina Hill was an enormous woman who ate for Britain.

She would visit me regularly at the police station and talk non-stop about her favourite pastime – eating!

Georgina never got offered seconds when dining because she usually ate for hours!

However, her obesity was beginning to cause her considerable health problems and was becoming a serious worry to her family.

As luck would have it, they struck out and won several thousand pounds on the lottery.

They booked the predictable sunshine holidays and cars, but the family also decided to contact a specialist cosmetic surgeon and arrange a private consultation for Georgina about a tummy tuck.

Having been encouraged by her family that this was the way to go, Georgina agreed to have the surgeon operate and make her a new woman.

After successfully going under the knife, Georgina received three 'get well' cards!

One was from her beloved husband Wullie!

One was from the cosmetic surgeon who performed her successful operation!

And the other one was from Brian in the Burns Unit thanking her for his new ears and the complete rebuild of his arse!

Bloody Witch Doctor

· · ·

Whilst on traffic patrol duty one night with my partner, I had occasion to stop a car being driven erratically by a young man in the city centre.

We pulled him over and, as we suspected, he was under the influence of alcohol.

We arrested him and conveyed him to the central police station, where we carried out the procedure pertaining to a drink-driver.

The young driver, who turned out to be a student at one of the local universities, was given the opportunity of providing a blood sample, which would be taken by a doctor, or urine.

The student opted to provide blood and the police surgeon was contacted to attend.

Now, the police surgeon is a qualified GP who has a practice but is also on call to work for the police in any situation where a doctor's expertise is required.

As we sat in the doctor's room in the station awaiting his arrival, I was completing the forms required and the young student, who by this time had sobered up quite a bit due to the shock of being arrested, was informing me that he had been to a students' union party and genuinely didn't intend to drink and drive.

We were still chatting when I was informed of the arrival of the police surgeon.

I remained with the student while my colleague left the room to see the doctor.

As it turned out, the doctor was new and one of the first

black doctors who was to become a regular on call with the central police station, named Dr Mutu.

The door opened and in came Dr Mutu.

The student immediately sat upright in his chair and his relaxed facial expression changed to one of total apprehension.

'Hello, I'm Dr Mutu and I am here to examine you and take a sample of your blood, which I'm informed you have agreed to provide.'

To the surprise of everyone present, the student said, 'Not on your life, Sammy Davis! You're not taken any blood from me!'

'Calm down now,' said Dr Mutu. 'I'm a doctor! You won't feel a thing!'

'You're darn tootin' I won't, 'cause you're no' touching me! Now, do a drum roll and beat it – I want a proper doctor, not some refugee as black as two in the morning who's just arrived here in a banana boat!' blasted the rude student.

As he sat back down with a genuine look of extreme fear on his face, I tried to calm him down. 'C'mon, man, cool it and don't start acting stupid. You've been fine up until now!' I said reassuringly.

But he interrupted me. 'Aye, right up until *he* came in! I mean, how do I know he's a doctor? Let him prove it!' he said, his voice quivering with genuine fear.

'I *am* a doctor!' answered Dr Mutu.

'Well, prove it, then. Let's see some medical certificates. I mean, I've proved to the police I'm a student – I gave them my university student ID card and I also gave them my driving licence to prove I'm a qualified driver. So let me see your ID!' demanded the student, becoming more nervous.

'But I *am* a doctor!' reiterated Dr Mutu, annoyed that his qualifications were being called into question. 'Now, I'm here to take blood from you!'

'Aye, right, with a bloody spear! I don't think so, "chief" – away back to your village and shrink a few more skulls for the tourists!' cried the student, who by now had lost the plot and was petrified. He continued, 'Just climbed down out a tree and thinks I'm going to let him stick spears in me! Or is it darts you're using tonight, chief? No way, big man, I'm not letting him near me!'

Dr Mutu was visibly shocked by this reaction from the student, but was still trying to plead his case. 'I am a doctor.'

My partner and I were in pain, trying not to laugh at the antics of them both, particularly the quiet unassuming student of fifteen minutes ago who was now acting as if the station had become Rorke's Drift and we'd been surrounded by Zulus.

I was trying to restrain the student and calm him down, but he was still rambling, 'It's all right for you two, saying calm down, but you're not the one being faced with *him*!' he said, almost crying with fear.

In the meantime, Dr Mutu was still reiterating, 'But I am a doctor.' He then looked to me for confirmation, emphasising his words, 'Tell him, officer – *I am a doctor*!'

'Aye, a bloody witch doctor!' replied the student. 'Show me some proof, then. Let me see your medical certificates! C'mon, then, show me!'

'I don't carry my medical certificates about with me,' said Dr Mutu. 'You just have to believe me when I tell you that I am a doctor!'

'Sorry, chief, not good enough!' replied the student.

Finally, after all the commotion from the student and Dr Mutu, coupled with the now hysterical laughter of my partner and me, the door opened and in walked the duty officer.

'What the hell is going on in here? You can be heard all along the corridor!' he yelled.

'Idi Amin here is blowing smoke signals out his arse as well as his ears!' responded the student.

'You just keep quiet,' I said. 'You're in enough bother!'

I stepped outside with the duty officer and explained what had taken place. Fortunately he had a good sense of humour.

However, the student continued to refuse the blood test and was detained in custody, pending release later that morning.

Dr Mutu went home after a cup of coffee and probably prescribed himself some Valium for the rest of the week to help get him down off the ceiling.

Later, while sitting discussing the hilarious antics of the student, and particularly Dr Mutu, the duty officer remarked, 'It's only been a matter of time. I've been waiting for it, from some drunk, but I didn't expect it from him – he looked a fairly decent educated young man.!'

Mind you, he'll definitely think twice about drinking and driving again!

Speed Camera Excuses

. . .

'There was a strong wind behind my car which pushed me along and caused me to exceed the speed limit.'

Jackie Barnes

. . .

I'm reminded of a story about auld Jack, an alcoholic who was recovering from a liver transplant and went into his local hardware shop asking for a bottle of methylated spirits.

The shopkeeper looked at Jack suspiciously and said, 'C'mon, Jack, I can't give you a bottle of meths – you're just out of hospital and have a serious drink problem!'

Jack assured the shopkeeper he was doing some DIY in his house and needed it to clean paintbrushes!

'But, Jack, I can't trust you – you have a drink problem!' he said.

Jack came storming back at him, 'Look! If my wife came into your shop and asked for a bottle of meths, you'd give it to her, wouldn't you?'

The shopkeeper thought for a moment, then sheepishly conceded to Jack's explanation. 'You're right, Jack. I'm sorry for not believing in you!'

As he bent down to pick up a bottle from a shelf, Jack said, 'You couldn't give me one out the cooler, could you?'

The Provident Insurance Man

· · ·

My uncle John was a typical Glesca character and I couldn't write another book without including him in it.

Several years ago, the Provident Insurance man would call at his house and collect the weekly death insurance policy payments.

One night my aunt Morag was serving up the evening meal to the family, seated around the dining table, when there was a knock at the door.

Uncle John got up and went out to answer it.

He returned a moment later and said, 'Morag, it's the Provi man looking for his money!'

Aunt Morag replied, 'Well, you better tell him I don't have it and he'll just need to come back next week.'

'Why not, then? Where's the money?' Uncle John asked.

'On the table, John – ye're frigging eating it!' she responded.

Uncle John looked at the spread of food on the table and all his kids eating, before returning to the door and informing the Provident Insurance collector, 'You'll need tac come back next week, pal, we've nae money.'

'But you said that last week, Mr Docherty, and this is your death policy after all,' said the Provi man.

To which Uncle John replied, 'Well, I'll tell ye whit, son. If I'm still alive next week, I'll make sure you get paid double, OK?'

He then closed the door on the stunned Provident Insurance man before returning to his meal.

John Wayne or Just a Pain

. . .

One of my many nutcase visitors to the office was a man in his late fifties named Tam 'Roy' Rogers, who had nothing better to do but call in every time I was on the nightshift and relate the same story, over and over again, about his cowboy screen hero, John Payne, not to be confused with *my* favourite western screen hero, John Wayne!

In he would come, straight from the pub and always laden down with carrier bags of groceries, which made me think he went shopping then straight to the pub and then afforded me his final visit of the night before heading for the Ponderosa.

Down the bags would go and he'd be off at a tangent.

'Do you remember John Payne? Man, he was something else. Remember that picture? I forget the name of it now but it will come to me. Anyway, he was the sheriff of the town and he was just married and all these bad guys that he had put in prison were getting released that day and making their way back to the town to get him. Now Jack Elam was one of them. He was usually bad and they nick-named him "Black Jack", because he had "Pontoon" eyes. Y'know – one was happy and the other one had gone for a twist, and—'

I had to interrupt him, 'Hold on a minute! That's Gary Cooper you're referring too, not John Payne!'

'No, no, no!' he said. 'See, he walks into the middle of the town street and he has to take them all on himself, because the rest of the town folk and his young bride, Gene Kelly, have all buggered off leaving him, but he—'

'Wait a minute! You're talking absolute mince. That's *High Noon* you're describing with Gary Cooper and Grace Kelly, I'm telling you!'

'Don't be silly, Mr Morris,' he said. 'Gary Cooper was the magician who wore a stupid hat and would throw his hands out in front of himself and say, "Just like that!" You must remember him!'

'I *do* remember him!' I said. 'That's *Tommy* Cooper!'

'No, Mr Morris!' he said convincingly. '*Tommy* Cooper was the guy that played for the Rangers at football!'

'What medication are you on?' I replied. 'That's complete and utter rubbish – it was *Davie* Cooper who played for Rangers!'

He continued in the same vein, 'Wrong again, Mr Morris – he was in the last stand at the Alamo along with David Bowie!'

'You're talking total bollocks, Roy. That was Davie Crockett, not Davie Cooper, and he was played by John Wayne! And it was Jim Bowie in the Alamo, not David Bowie!'

To which he said confidently, 'Correct, that's what I have been saying all along, Mr Morris. John Wayne stood in the middle of the deserted town and called all the bad guys out to face him!'

Roy then stood in front of me like a gunslinger with his arms by his sides and then pulled his jacket back, as if to display his holstered gun.

He then stared me straight in the eye, daring me to do likewise and go for the draw. I could see something in his pocket, but I couldn't make it out.

As I made a slight movement, he went for the draw and produced a small bottle of Coca-Cola, which he pointed at me before placing it on my office counter.

'That's for you, Sheriff!' he said. 'Have a drink on me!'

Obviously my reward for putting up with him!

Unfortunately I had endured about enough of his wind-up descriptions of the films starring John 'bloody' Payne, David Bowie and Tommy Cooper that I told him to 'head them up and roll them out before I come round the front of the office and put my size-nine "Doc Holliday" boots up your horse's arse and give it a real *Rawhide*!'

As he picked up his message bags and walked to the door, he turned to face me and said, 'See you tomorrow night, Mr Morris, and I'll tell you about a film called *The Quiet Man* with Brian Connolly and Ken Scott!'

I took the bait and responded immediately, 'I think you mean *The Big Man* with Billy Connolly and Ken Stott.'

He gave a wry smile and said, 'Now, Mr Morris, are you winding me up?'

'Not at all,' I said. 'I'm rolling, rolling, rolling, and you're being a right wee Rowdy Yates tonight!'

He then winked and said, 'My stagecoach is due, so I'll bid you adios, amigo!'

He then disappeared out the front door into the moonlit street.

Oh, boy! Do I need counselling or what?

Chat-Up Lines

· · ·

This is the point where I supply you with some of my expertise in the art of chatting up the opposite sex and, basically, don't do as I do, or say, for that matter, but try it for yourself.

There I'd be, strutting my stuff in my white suit, moving around the dance floor effortlessly like a Dalek.

My dance partner was three dress sizes bigger than she should be and bursting out all over!

During a 'smoochie' dance, I glanced at the label on the neck of her top – it said '22'! So I naturally assumed that was her age.

Just when I felt the time was right, I struck with my first chat-up line.

'I'll tell you this, Thelma – you don't sweat much for a fat burd!'

Failing to obtain the desired response I was expecting, I followed this up with next one on my hit list.

'Do you like babies? Fancy going halfers with me for one?'

But I soon found out the best chat-up line that definitely worked with the burds, especially from the South Ayrshire area, was when you took them to one side and said, 'Slip yer hand into my trouser pocket and feel what I have for you!'

Seconds after she'd put her hands around it, you were up the road for a good night and guaranteed to have a piping-hot breakfast the following morning.

'What was it?' I hear you ask, or is it that too obvious?

'Simple, my dear Watson' – an electricity power card!

Congratulations

. . .

A ned was caught breaking into a shop, but like most of his type, he pled not guilty, allowing him more time in the hope that he might get off on a technicality.

To defend him in court, he had employed the services of the best lawyer that money could buy – taxpayers' money, that is.

The day of his trial arrived, at Glasgow Sheriff Court, where he continued with his plea of not guilty and as a result the trial commenced.

First in the witness box was the police officer who had apprehended him.

'You are Constable James Reid of Strathclyde Police 'D' Division based at Baird Street police station – is that correct?' asked the procurator fiscal.

The officer paused for a moment, before answering, 'Well, yes and no!'

This response was met with some bewilderment from the fiscal, who stood staring with a puzzled look on his face.

At that, the officer continued, 'Well, you see, I was promoted to the rank of sergeant yesterday and I am now based at "G" Division, Govan.'

A look of relief came over the procurator fiscal, who congratulated the officer on his promotion.

This was soon interrupted by the sheriff, who was a little slow in the uptake. He asked the fiscal to please explain what was happening.

'I'm just congratulating the police witness on his recent promotion to sergeant!' explained the fiscal.

'Oh, I see,' said the sheriff, who then turned his attention to the officer and said, 'Please accept my congratulations also!'

'Thank you, m'lord,' responded the officer.

He was then led through his evidence by the procurator fiscal and things were looking very bleak for the accused.

It was then the turn of the defence solicitor to take the floor.

'Well, *Sergeant* Reid,' said the solicitor, 'before I begin my cross-examination, may I likewise take the opportunity to congratulate you on your recent promotion!'

At this point the accused leapt to his feet and shouted across the court at his defence agent, 'Aw, for fuck's sake – I'm pleading guilty!'

What's He Like?

• • •

Whilst walking through a busy shopping mall one day, a young boy came running over to me with tears in his eyes and said, 'I've lost my daddy!'

'What's yer daddy like, son?' I asked him.

The young boy thought for a moment then said, 'Horse racing and drinking whisky!'

A reply that describes an awful lot of daddies in Glesca!

Clockwork

· · ·

A deputy divisional commander looked out from his office and called to his secretary, 'Excuse me, Miss Jones, but can you come into my office for a minute and look at my clock, please?'

He then went back inside and closed the door.

Moments later, Miss Jones knocked on his door.

'Come in, Miss Jones,' answered the deputy commander.

As Miss Jones entered the office, she saw the deputy commander standing there with his trousers and underpants at his ankles, exposing his privates.

Miss Jones blushed and turned her head away in total embarrassment and said, 'Deputy Commander! I thought you said to come into your office and look at your clock!'

To which the deputy commander replied, 'I did! Don't you think it would look good with a face and a pair of hands around it?'

The Mach 3 Razor Test

· · ·

A policewoman who swallowed a Mach 3 ladies' razor was found not only to be responsible for having circumcised her lover, but had cut two fingers off a passing acquaintance and given her shift inspector a hair lip.

But she still managed to have five more shaves!

The Wedding Party

· · ·

A young couple from the East End of Glasgow were getting married.

It was a lovely church wedding, followed by a reception at a city centre bar.

Unfortunately for the couple, they both came from very rough backgrounds and there was a bit of an ongoing feud between their families.

Inevitably, after the drink started flowing at the reception, things became heated between both parties and a fight broke out. The resident bouncers at the bar/diner tried to defuse the situation but to no avail and, as a result, they summoned the assistance of the local police.

The first cops to arrive on the scene tried in vain to separate the bride's brother and the best man, who were physically locked in combat, but found that the other guests on both sides were encouraging them to continue with their battle.

With no solution in sight, the cops called for more assistance, which resulted in the arrival of the support unit.

This is a minibus full of uniformed officers and cruelly referred to 'Rent a Mob', but more often as 'Rent a Riot'.

The bar was engulfed by a sea of black uniforms, who quickly asserted their authority by force. However, they were unable to separate the two members of the wedding party still locked in mortal combat.

Joe Logan, the big sergeant, stepped forward to use physical strength to pull them apart, but had great difficulty as the bride's mother pulled and jostled him from behind and shouted, 'Leave my son alane, ya big bastard! He's done fuck all!'

The sergeant tried several times to fend her off, but some of the other guests became involved and could clearly be heard shouting, 'Maw! Maw! Don't get involved – they'll gie ye the jail! Maw! Maw, please, Maw!'

At that, the mother committed the most despicable act of all by spitting in the sergeant's face.

This was a real grogger or, as we say, a 'soft poached egg', consisting of all forms of slime in a glue-like substance.

'That's it!' cried big Joe the sergeant. 'Jail the maw!'

On hearing this command, two cops rushed forward and grabbed the bride's mother, ushering her outside to the waiting police van.

Not the dignified exit she had intended, as she landed upside down at the door with her knickers in the air, screaming blue murder.

The sergeant finally arrested the two men at the centre of the disturbance and conveyed them to a city centre police station to be detained in custody.

However, he was shocked on his arrival when he saw a huge queue of prisoners at the charge desk.

It appeared that all the guests at the wedding had been apprehended.

'What are they all doing here?' asked Joe the sergeant.

'We were ordered to arrest them!' replied a young cop.

'Who gave the order to arrest them?' enquired Joe.

'*You* did!' replied the young cop, with a puzzled look on his face.

'What do you mean, *I* gave the order?' said Joe, now panicking.

To which the young cop replied, 'You did! You shouted out, "That's it! Jail them aw!"'

Joe quickly corrected him, 'I gave the order to "jail the maw"!' ('Maw' being a Glesca endearment for the mother).

Steven or Stephen?

• • •

A young cop attended a call to a house with regards to a domestic dispute.

As the police arrived, they were informed by the wife that her husband had left the house just prior to their arrival.

The young cop began to note some details and asked the wife her husband's particulars.

The wife gave his name as Steven, at which he asked her, 'Is that with a "v" or a "ph"?'

The wife looked at him with a puzzled expression on her face and replied rather condescendingly, 'Neither! It's with an "S"!'

This was surely one wife who didn't take her husband's name too seriously!

Get Them Off!

• • •

Whilst attending the Tulliallan Police College, it was the night of our qualifying dinner celebration.

Along with our instructors and the special invited guests, the college commandant and his wife, we all assembled at the local golf club, where our meal was being served up.

Prior to the big night, I had been approached by Inspector John Elliot and given the task of saying something on behalf of my colleagues and thanking our distinguished guest, the commandant, and his wife.

After an excellent meal, it was my moment to stand up and address my assembled fellow students, the instructors and special VIP guests.

I started off with the following: 'Earlier tonight, I was instructed by Inspector John Elliot to attend at the commandant's house and, in the absence of the commandant, I was given the privilege of escorting his wife to this evening's celebration. As I arrived at the house and rang the doorbell, I was invited inside by his wife. However, nothing could have prepared me for the events I was about to encounter, "Good evening, Constable Morris!. Do come in," she said, as she beckoned me to follow her inside. Once inside, she continued, "Do I call you Constable Morris all night, or do you have a first name?"

' "If it pleases you, ma'am, call me Harry!' I replied.

' "OK, Harry!" she said. "I'd like you to do something for me and I would appreciate it if you would follow my instructions to the letter! Do you understand me?" she asked.

' "I certainly do, ma'am!' I replied, wondering what was coming next.

' "Right, Harry, without arguing about it, I would like you to take off my evening dress and put it over the chair!' she ordered me!

' "But, ma'am!" I protested vigorously.

' "Do it please, Harry!" she said, demanding my obedience. I reluctantly removed her evening dress and placed it over the chair as instructed. "Thank you, Harry!" she said. "Now, will you please remove my suspender belt and my black silk stockings?" she added, with a hint of a nervous quiver in her voice.

' "But, ma'am!" I reiterated. "This is—"

' "Will you please do as I ask, Harry, without arguing?" she said, exerting her authority. "This is not exactly easy for me either!"

' "Ye're right, ma'am. I apologise." At that, I removed her suspenders and stockings.'

Now, by this time the instructors seated around the table didn't know what to do and, even worse, they didn't know what was coming next. My fellow students were physically choking and stuffing napkins in their mouths in an obvious attempt to hold back their laughter.

However, not intimidated by the instructors squirming in their seats or their staring eyes, I continued with my story.

' "Thank you, Harry. Now, please remove my bra and pants!" she instructed me.

' "Are you sure about this, ma'am?" I asked, seeking reassurance.

' "Do it, please!" she screamed.

' "OK! OK!" I replied. "No need to loose yer head, ma'am. I know ye're embarrassed about it, but so am I!" At that, I whipped off her bra and pants with the minimum of fuss and effort. Having performed everything she had asked of me and removed all of her clothes, she looked at me straight in face and said, ' "If I ever catch you wearing my clothes again, I'll be forced to report you to the college commandant!" '

A reply, I might add, that was greeted with heavy sighs of relief from the assembled instructors.

Oh! And the commandant of the police college!!

You're Not Dead?

• • •

My eighty-year-old mother is sometimes lacking in subtlety.

One day, whilst walking around the local Asda with her, we bumped into my uncle John, whom she hadn't seen or heard from for some time.

'Crikey, John, it's that long since I've seen you, I was sure you were dead!'

To which Uncle John replied, 'Not at all! Doctors Whyte and Mackay are looking after me.'

To which my mother repeated, 'That's the honest truth – I thought you were dead!'

'Well,' said Uncle John, 'as you can see, I'm not, but then again . . . I *am* looking for directions to the spirit section!'

Margaret Dale

• • •

Several days ago I learned that an old friend, Margaret Dale, had passed away in her sleep after a long illness.

I met Margaret many years ago when the Police Federation employed her as the office cleaner and 'mammy' to them all.

Every morning, I would arrive at the back door to the office on my police motorcycle and Margaret would have a hot breakfast of bacon, sausage, egg, toast and tea ready for me to enjoy.

This was an early morning ritual for a long time and, in return, I would entertain Margaret with my stories and jokes.

Margaret would love our morning chats and a right good laugh.

However, like all things in life, we move on and my visits were restricted, only seeing Margaret in my fleeting visits to the Federation office.

It was during one of these visits that I learned that Margaret was very unwell and was in an isolated room in the Victoria Infirmary in Glasgow.

I decided to make some time available and go to the Vicky and pay Margaret a surprise visit, to try and cheer her up.

As I made my way along a corridor, trying to find Margaret's room, a nurse approached and asked if she could help me.

'I'm looking for Margaret Dale,' I told her.

She directed me to a room further along the corridor,

then enquired if I was a member of her family. I informed her I wasn't but I was a close friend.

The nurse apologised and said that visiting was restricted to close family members only.

As I reluctantly made to leave, I saw the nurse enter another room, so I quickly made my way along the corridor and entered Margaret's room.

Margaret's face lit up with the smile I was accustomed to seeing during my morning visits to the office for breakfast.

I put my arms around her and gave her a big cuddle and a peck on the cheek.

'How did you get in here?' she asked. 'I'm not allowed visitors!'

'Easy-peasy!' I replied. 'I told them I was your gynaecologist!'

This prompted spontaneous laughter from Margaret.

As I sat there beside of her hospital bed, telling her jokes and stories to try and amuse her, it was just like old times again, only without the bacon-and-egg breakfast.

Margaret loved to laugh and lived life to the full with her husband Alex, to whom she was married for over twenty-five years.

I don't know if it was her laughter that drew the attention or just a routine visit, but a young doctor entered her room and was surprised to see me seated there.

With a clipboard in his hand, he asked, 'Excuse me, but can I help you?'

It was time to make a hasty retreat.

'Who exactly are you?' he enquired.

I couldn't resist it as I got up from my seat, held my hand out to shake his and said, 'Dr Morris at your cervix. I'm Mrs Dale's very own private gynaecologist!'

I then looked over at Margaret and, as I winked at her, I said, 'Your fanny is perfect, Mrs Dale. Nothing to worry about there!'

As I slipped out the door and made my way back along the corridor, all I could hear was Margaret hooting with laughter.

A fond memory!

Dedicated to Alex and family.

No Age Limits

. . .

George Hyslop, an ageing inspector soon to retire from the police force, announced to colleagues on his shift that his retirement party would also be his stag night because, after twelve years as a widower, he had decided to remarry.

Everyone offered him congratulations.

'Who is the lucky woman, then?' they asked him.

'Mary Brown!' he proudly announced.

His shift personnel were stunned. Mary Brown was a young probationer policewoman.

This prompted one of the officers to ask, 'What about the age difference, George?'

To which George replied with a straight face, while sipping on his gin and tonic, 'If she dies, she dies!'

Aye Right, Harry!

· · ·

Having suffered a severe back injury, I was prescribed a deep-heat cream rub from the doctor.

The instructions on the box stated, 'For best results, warm up the affected area before massaging/rubbing the cream on.'

With a massage parlour in the area nearby, I decided to pay it a visit and have the cream massaged on professionally.

I entered and paid my money to the receptionist and explained about my cream. She directed me to a changing room to undress and issued me with a large bath towel to wear.

Thereafter, I was shown to a small cubicle by a blonde masseuse and told to lie on the bed.

As I lay on my stomach, the masseuse entered the room and began to massage the cream into my back, stopping briefly to apply a heat lamp to the affected area.

When the treatment was finished, I got dressed and left the premises to return to my car, parked nearby.

Whilst sitting in my car and adjusting my seat, totally unaware of what was happening all around me, I was given the fright of my life as my driver's window was rattled.

I looked up to see a police colleague standing at my car door.

'What the hell are you up to, Harry boy? We're doing a stakeout on that place!' he said, surprised at my appearance there.

Try as hard as I might to convince him that my visit was purely medical, professional and genuine, he responded by saying, 'Aye right, Harry! And if pigs could fly, you'd be a squadron leader!'

Recognition at Last
· · ·

Walking around a car boot sale, I was delighted to find an old *Morris's Motorcycle News Magazine* I had written about twenty years ago, while in the police force, for a children's charity.

Eagerly picking it up, I thought to myself, 'Recognition at last! I'm for sale in a car boot.' I asked the price.

'You can have it for fifty pence,' said the stallholder.

My expression dropped as I thought about all the hard work I had put into writing it, only to learn that it was being sold for such a paltry sum all these years later.

Sensing my hesitation, the stallholder said, 'Oh, all right, you can have it for twenty-five pence, then.'

I looked at him with utter contempt and said, 'No, thanks, mate. I've read it.'

Then under my breath I muttered, 'Ya bastard!'

Offer He Couldn't Refuse

· · ·

I received a call from Andy, an off-duty police officer requiring urgent assistance. However, he would not specify over the telephone why or what it was.

I immediately attended at the address given by Andy, aware that this was not his home address, and on my arrival he opened the door to me.

'Quick, Harry, come in, come in!' he pleaded.

As I entered the living room, I saw three children under the age of five playing with toys, completely oblivious to my appearance.

Now, I know what you're thinking. Were there any Gary Glitter or Michael Jackson records on the hi-fi turntable?

Not at all. The explanation was as simple as big Andy, for getting himself into this position.

It appears he was out drinking with some colleagues on his shift and they progressed to the 'Charles Manson' (dancin').

Whilst there he met, began smooching and fell head over heels with a big blonde goddess who posed the question, 'How would you like to come home with me and have my babies?'

Andy didn't need to be asked twice. He was infatuated by her.

However, when he awoke in the morning, his blonde goddess had buggered off, abandoning him with her three children.

Hooray for the Social Work Department, who came to Andy's rescue!

Jumping Without a Net

· · ·

When Alfie went on a drinking spree, he would disappear for days on end, making fleeting appearances at a relative's home every now and again for somewhere to rest his head and borrow more beer money to continue with his binge!

Having arrived at the house of one of his many concerned sisters, he made his way into the spare bedroom and crashed out, instantly falling into a deep sleep.

His sister immediately phoned around the other family members to let them know he was there and asking what to do.

It was agreed she should lock the bedroom door to prevent him from leaving, thus giving the rest of the sisters time to get to her house to try and speak with him about seeking help with his drinking problem.

However, in the interim period, Alfie had woken from his drunken state, totally unaware of where he was.

As he tried to open the bedroom door, he found his exit hindered by a lock on the outside.

Unable to get out of the room, Alfie began to sweat profusely and, in a panic, he went over to the bedroom window and looked out as the rain poured from the skies relentlessly. It was obvious to Alfie that he was in a top-floor apartment with no other apparent escape route, except for a balcony situated to the right of the bedroom window.

Alfie tried desperately to think of an escape plan, when suddenly it became crystal clear. He would climb out the window, shimmy his way along the window ledge until he could reach over and grab hold of the balcony railing, then dreep down from the top one, catching hold of the one on the floor below as he fell, then dreep from that one, catching the next one down as he fell, and so on until he finally reached the ground.

'Simple!' he thought. 'James Bond does it all the time – it'll be a dawdle!'

Alfie pulled himself up on to the windowsill and, opening the bedroom window, he climbed outside on to the ledge as the torrential rain quickly drenched him.

Hanging on to the window frame, Alfie began slowly and tentatively manoeuvring his way along the ledge towards the balcony.

He stretched his arms out, reaching for the rail, and managed to get a good hold before placing his feet firmly on the bottom of the rail.

'So far, so good!' he thought.

Now for the next step of letting go his grip of the rail, dropping down and grasping hold of the next safety rail on the balcony below!

As Alfie looked down at the ground from his precarious position on the top-floor balcony, he took time to compose himself, taking several deep breaths to try and calm his nerves.

Just at that point his sister, who was unaware of Alfie's acrobatics outside, was pacing up and down in her living room, puffing away relentlessly on a cigarette, pondering the next step when the other members of her family arrived.

Suddenly she looked out the window and saw Alfie hanging on like grim death to the railing outside.

Shocked by this terrifying sight, she let out a huge scream, 'Aaarrgghh!'

This was so loud and screechy, it completely startled Alfie, who got such a fright he accidentally released his tight grip of the railing.

His sister looked on in horror as Alfie's face distorted to a look of absolute fear as he disappeared from view, falling backwards and rapidly downwards.

She ran to the window to see the outcome of his fall but, unable to see where he had landed, she ran for the outside door and rushed downstairs to give assistance.

As she reached the ground floor and ran outside to the back court, fearing and expecting the worse, she looked for her brother Alfie's broken body.

To her astonishment, there was no trace of Alfie!

Had she imagined all of it?

What could possibly have happened to him?

Well, I can confirm it actually did happen, but due to Alfie's drunken, relaxed condition, coupled with the torrential rain which had made the drying green very soft and muddy, Alfie had landed and slid his way down the muddy embankment to the bottom before getting up and legging it as fast as he could.

He sustained absolutely no injuries whatsoever and by the time his sister had appeared at the back court to find him, he assures me he was in the nearest boozer along the road with a large whisky and a beer chaser sitting in front of him!

Trying to calm his nerves, no doubt!

Alfie was none the worse for his death-defying leap and is still alive today to tell the tale!

So, Pierce Brosnan, or should I say Daniel Craig, you had better beware!

Private Sports

. . .

After a competitive game of football for the police divisional team, we were back in the changing room getting undressed to enter the showers for a well-earned soak and wash.

The cop next to me was Davie Hamilton, an ex-Royal Marine, who had joined the police after being discharged from the armed forces.

I couldn't help but notice he had what appeared to be writing tattooed on the shaft of his penis.

I thought it might have been an army thing (you know what the Royal Marines are like – 'Death before dishonour', 'Ladies before gents', 'Age before beauty' and all that crap), or maybe his wife's name, so before asking him about it, I tried to see what it said, without making my curiosity to obvious and appearing like George Michael in a public toilet.

Then I read what I thought was 'AIDS'!

'Why have you got "AIDS" tattooed on your boaby?' I asked.

He looked at me for a moment and then said, 'It's actually "ADIDAS", the sports brand, but unfortunately it's only really legible when my penis is erect!'

Not wishing to take it any further, or have him confirm it, I decided to accept his explanation!

However, I would have thought 'LE COQ SPORTIF' would have been more appropriate tattoo for that part of his anatomy!

Andy's Hit and Run!

· · ·

Whilst the Celtic folk band I belonged to were touring the Netherlands, we had just finished the final concert of the tour and had packed all our instruments and luggage on to our tour bus to make a mad dash for the Rotterdam ferry, on the first part of our homeward journey to Harwich.

Andy volunteered to drive the bus on this leg of the journey, which was mostly motorway, while the rest of the guys had a well-earned sleep in the back.

I sat in the front passenger seat as we drove along the motorway, occasionally coming up against heavy traffic and having to slow right down.

Due to these delays, we were cutting it fine to catch our ferry so, as soon as we got past the heavy traffic, Andy put the pedal to the metal and we sped on our way, travelling at the maximum speed limit to make up some time.

We carried on like this for some time until we were a few kilometres from the ferry exit road and a build-up of more traffic.

Just as we were slowing down and the lights were illuminating the motorway, I saw a very large bird skimming over the top of the cars immediately in front of us.

I briefly thought to myself, 'That's brilliant!' and was about to mention it to the others when it suddenly struck me that we were driving a bus, which is much higher than a car and, lo and behold, before I could open my mouth to speak – crash! bang! wallop! – the large bird flew into the front of our bus, smashing the windscreen. It then went hurtling over the top.

Andy hadn't seen it coming and got such a fright, his

bomb doors opened and he shat himself, followed by the outburst, 'Whit the f-f-fuck was that?!'

Quick as a flash, I replied, 'Crikey, Andy, you've just hit a hitch-hiker! Keep going!'

And guess what?

He did!

By the time we reached the ferry terminal Andy was a nervous wreck, almost in tears and totally minging, I might add!

Now I don't know if diarrhoea runs in your genes, but it was definitely running in his denim jeans, that's for sure!

'What are we going to do, Harry?' he asked.

'What are *we* going to do?' I thought to myself.

'Excuse me, Andy, what's this "we"? It was *you* that hit her!' I said, distancing myself from any blame.

He then thought for a moment, then said, 'Her?! Don't tell me it wis a burd Ah hit?!'

'Aye!' I said with a straight face. 'You might have even killed her for all we know! I mean to say, just look at the damage she did to our bus!'

As Andy's eyes began to fill up, I realised it wasn't funny any more and he was taking me seriously, so I said, 'It's OK, Andy, it was only an old bird.'

'It doesn't matter whit her age is, I've hit her!' he replied. 'I cannae believe it. It's an auld bird I've hit noo – I might even have killed her! When you said it was a hitch-hiker, I just automatically assumed it was a guy, now it's an auld woman—'

I interrupted him, 'Naw, naw, naw, ya diddy – it was just an old feathery bird. You know, like a big seagull!'

He paused for a moment, staring at me, his eyes filled with tears, as I stared back at him with a mischievous grin on my face. He then shook his head and said, 'You are a sick, sick man, Harry Morris!'

One by one, the other band members burst out laughing, prompting Andy to see the funny side (eventually)!

However, as a final goodwill gesture, once on board the ferry, I went to the shops and purchased some new duty-free underwear for him to change into!

Oh, and a new pair of denim jeans, for as we all know, diarrhoea is messy! I really do have a heart!

The Alibi
• • •

I received a call to a house with a complaint regarding the neighbours leaving their bedroom curtains open at night while they indulged in explicit sexual intercourse.

I attended at the house in question and knocked on the door.

After a few moments the husband opened it.

I made him aware of the complaint that I had received regarding him and his wife having explicit sex in the house, with the bedroom curtains wide open.

To which the man responded, 'Well, I can assure you, sir, it wasn't me! 'Cause I was working a nightshift last night!'

He reminded me of the guy whose long-term girlfriend informed him she was having a baby, and he responded by saying, 'Are you sure it's yours?'

Toffee Legs Tribute

. . .

In the early seventies, Chief Superintendent Henderson controlled the South 'D' Division. This incorporated Craigie Street HQ, Castlemilk, Pollokshaws and the Gorbals.

'Toffee Legs', as he was affectionately nicknamed, was one of the old school and ruled with an iron fist.

He wanted his pound of flesh and if you were working overtime, you had to be seen pounding your beat and earning your extra payment.

He would also regularly turn up at the station and go out on patrol, speaking with and encouraging the men patrolling their areas.

I must confess to having had a great respect for him as my divisional commander.

He would meet you for the first time, in the office or out on the street, and maybe not see you for another two or three weeks but, when he did, he would address you by your first name.

His memory for names and faces was incredible.

He had a great affinity with his officers and liked to be involved in the thick of things, leading from the front as he regularly arrested anyone causing disorderly behaviour in public.

I remember speaking with a showman at Glasgow Green who asked me about him and told me how much he was respected by the show people. He then related a story about a young Toffee Legs physically dragging two and three trouble-making neds at a time to the gates and ejecting them from the park.

He also had a rule in D Division that all officers patrolling the area would, after 11 p.m. (public houses closed at 10 p.m. in those days), stop and check all cars or pedestrians moving or making their way through the divisional area.

Believe me, this had a great crime-prevention effect in the division.

It also prompted a few of the older cops to supply their sons with taxi money to prevent them walking home and being stopped by the police.

A lot of people might think of his methods of policing as draconian, but I'm positive the effect it had on our crime figures was important and if a call went out for police assistance, a disturbance or housebreaking, the response the call would receive would be immediate as officers from all parts of the division raced to get there first, such was our eagerness to detect and arrest offenders.

This, I believe, was also largely due to the influence of Toffee Legs and his unbelievable enthusiasm, which he displayed at all times.

He would never ask you to do anything that he wouldn't or couldn't do himself, such was his attitude.

Finally, I would also like to say that at fifty-four years of age I saw him take on a police officer, at least twenty years his junior, at press-ups in the front office at Pollokshaws police station.

The younger officer, who was taunting him about how fit he was for his age, was a regular jogger – or runner as we would refer to them back in the early seventies – and would run to and from his place of work daily.

Suffice to say he was physically fit.

However, not fit enough, for not only did Toffee Legs beat his much younger colleague, but he finished off by doing ten one-armed press-ups just to rub salt in the wound of his challenger.

Sadly, Chief Superintendent Henderson passed away several years ago, but his memory will never be forgotten – by the many neds he arrested in his time or by the many young police officers, such as myself, whose careers he most definitely influenced.

He also showed me that policing the community in general could be as enjoyable as eating toffee!

Gentlemen Joggers

· · ·

One night at about half past twelve, I received a call to the Cathkin Braes, an area which was becoming more and more frequented by homosexual men.

The complaint was, as usual, of men acting suspiciously or, as we would refer to it, 'grown men sword-fencing on the Braes'!

As far as I was concerned, if they were up in the Braes they were well out of the way of the public; however, I attended.

I parked the police car and was having a look around when I saw the figure of a man in his late fifties, dressed in a vest and pants, in the grassed area among some trees.

I beckoned him over and enquired what he was doing out at this time of night, dressed in his underwear, socks and shoes.

Quick as a flash, he responded, 'I'm a jogger out jogging!'

'It's a bit late to be doing that, sir!' I said. 'And you're not exactly sporty-looking or dressed in sportswear, are you?'

'Well, I am and I run like this all the time and no one has ever complained before,' he responded.

'Well, sir! The complaint I have is not about joggers – it's about grown men acting suspiciously. D'you know what I'm saying, sir? This is an area renowned for men engaging in homosexual activities.'

'Well, I can assure you, officer, I haven't seen anybody like that tonight!' he replied convincingly.

I looked at him, trying desperately not to laugh, then asked, 'Tell me, sir, do you always go out jogging in you underwear, Burberry socks and a pair of polished brown brogues?'

'Why? Is it a crime to run in my shoes?' he replied indignantly.

'No, sir, it's not, but your vest and pants are not normal!' I said. 'In fact, you look like you have come straight from Marks and Sparks' underwear department, rather than Greaves Sportswear!'

'Well, I can assure you I run like this regularly and have never been stopped yet by any of the police in Hamilton!' he replied.

'Hamilton?' I said, surprised. 'Are you telling me that you've run all the way from Hamilton to here, dressed like that?'

'And why not?' he responded. 'Are you calling me a liar?'

'Certainly not, sir!' I said. 'But I've put up with enough of your crap, so get back in there and get your clothes on now!'

'Are you deaf?' he asked. 'I've already told you, I'm out for a jog and you're keeping me late. My wife will be worried sick.'

'So you don't have a car parked near by either?' I asked.

'Certainly not! I've already told you, I ran here and I'll run all the way back home as well!' he replied.

Now, normally this guy and his sexual preferences would not bother me, but he was becoming a pain in *my* arse, so I told him to occupy a seat in the rear of the police car while I checked out his personal details.

While doing this, I noticed he was repeatedly looking at his watch, checking the time.

So, being the good public servant I was and ignoring his protest about wishing to run home, I insisted that I give him a lift a few miles along the road, shortening his journey towards Hamilton.

This was to make up for some of the time in which I had detained him and also to prevent his wife from getting too worried about him arriving home late!

He protested vigorously about holding me back from my other more important police duties, but I insisted.

When I finally stopped the car and let him out, I couldn't stop myself from laughing at his sport attire and his futile attempt at jogging.

It also wasn't a particularly warm October night to be out running in your underwear.

However, later while on my patrol, I did observe a very smart burgundy BMW motor car parked unattended in the Braes car park all night long, with, I might add, a neatly folded brown pin-stripe suit inside!

Guess who owned that, then?

Profumo Affair

• • •

During the John Profumo affair involving Christine Keeler and Mandy Rice-Davies, it was alleged that a senior Scotland Yard investigating officer remarked, 'Christine Keeler has more fingerprints up her arse than we have in our files!'

Pissed-Off Mic

· · ·

Whilst I was a member of a Scottish folk band, performing at a venue in Ayr, we were carrying out a routine sound check with our engineer.

Andy, our bagpipe player, was trying out a new radio microphone, fitted to his wrist, with what looked like a small pompom protruding downwards and running parallel with his playing fingers.

Now this was quite a technical piece of equipment, but if it were successful, it would allow Andy to step off stage and mingle with the audience while playing his great Highland bagpipes and the radio receiver would pick up his signal anywhere, out front of the venue, maintaining the sound levels.

After we had finished the check, the sound engineer echoed his delight with the outcome of Andy's radio microphone and was confident the experiment would be a huge success.

Satisfied with this, we all sat down and were enjoying a last-minute drink to relax us, prior to going on stage.

Andy decided to visit the toilet to pee or, as he put it, 'I'm off to siphon my python before we start the concert!'

As we looked over our set list for the performance, I spotted Steve, our sound engineer, with a puzzled expression on his face and twiddling frantically with the knobs on his sound desk.

'What's up, Steve?' I asked him.

'I'm not sure! Everything was perfect a minute ago and now all of a sudden I can hear some interference!'

'Like what?' I enquired.

Still twiddling the desk knobs, Steve said, 'It's like . . . a whooshing or a hissing sound – I can't figure it out!'

Just at that the sound changed to a crackling and a slight banging.

'What the hell is this now? Surely it's not a faulty sound desk? I'll re-check all the power leads and do a line check for it. I shouldn't take long!'

Now at this point, as a performer and the band manager, I was beginning to panic slightly and I had to go to the promoter and ask him for a short delay in starting the concert.

'Not a problem, Harry. That gives the punters more time to finish their drinks at the bar and re-order!' he replied.

I went back to see my sound engineer.

'What's happening, Steve? Any luck with the interference?'

Steve replied, 'I don't know what caused it, Harry, but it's stopped now!'

Relieved to hear this news, I sat down to finish my drink when Andy came over and sat down beside me and said, 'You'll never believe what I've just done, boss! I went for a piss and forgot to switch off my new radio mike and I've pissed all over it – the pompom was absolutely soaking!'

I just sat there looking at him, when the penny dropped and I realised what he was saying and started laughing.

Andy continued, 'It's all right, I think! I've dried it off.'

I then shouted over to Steve the engineer and said, 'I've solved the sound interference mystery, Steve. It was Andy pissing all over his brand new radio microphone, hence the whoosh and the crackling sound you heard!'

We all had a good laugh about it later.

By the way, so did every audience we ever performed to after that, 'cause I told them all about it.

However, it came in handy when we were performing at an open-air gig, because the pissy smell from his pompom microphone kept all the midges away from the rest of the band members.

Thereafter, when introducing the band, I would refer to Andy as playing the 'piss pipes' instead of the bagpipes!

Mind you, prior to my leaving the band, Andy was pissed most of the time anyway, and so were his bagpipes, come to think of it!

Hughie's Tortoise Room

· · ·

While growing up, I shared a room with my younger brother Hughie.

Both of us, I might add, were not exceptionally house-proud when it came to housework, particularly if it coincided with a game of football.

My long-suffering mother (wee Flo) gave up on us and refused to enter our room again to collect any washing until we got our act together and cleaned it up.

We had so much lying about you would have struggled to see the floor carpet. I kid you not – Lord Lucan could have been hiding in our room for years and we wouldn't have known.

Both being footballers, we had dirty football strips, socks, boots and minging jockstraps all lying about the floor.

We even offered to pay one of my younger sisters to tidy it up and she refused to enter the room without the required tropical injections needed to go abroad.

Finally my father, big Freddie, intervened.

'Both of you get into that room and don't come out until it's clean and tidy and doesn't require to have a health warning on the door before your mother goes in!'

Not about to argue with the big man, we entered our room armed with washing basket, Hoover, dusters, survival pack, garden strimmer and flamethrower.

Several hours later and umpteen black bin bags packed to the hilt, we discovered we had a carpet fitted to the floor.

The room was beginning to look spick and span, apart from the disgusting stale smell still circulating.

Two rose bouquet aerosols sprayed into the room with the door closed made absolutely no difference. It was still bowfin'! We even tried burning some incense sticks, but to no avail.

What could be causing this rancid pong? Then Hughie said, 'Maybe it's Torty. Maybe his bed needs cleaned!'

'Excuse me, but who is Torty and where did he come from?' I asked, thinking he had taken in a lodger without telling me and denying me my share of the rental proceeds.

'It's the school tortoise,' he replied. 'I volunteered to look after it during the hibernation period.'

'Since when?' I enquired, totally unaware of this arrangement.

'Since the summer holidays!' Then he added under his breath, 'Last year!'

'Last year?! And where is it now?' I asked, trying to remain calm.

'It was under my bed the last time Ah looked,' he replied.

At that point we got down on our knees and looked under his bed, where we found an empty shoebox that used to house Torty the tortoise.

'Where is he?' asked a surprised Hughie.

'He probably couldn't stand the smell of us two and buggered off months ago!' I replied sarcastically.

We started to look for him and it wasn't long before we found him, or should I say found the remains of his empty shell.

Torty was stuck to the floor in the corner, underneath Hughie's bed, like a British Rail pork pie (a hard shell with no meat)!

He had obviously decomposed over the previous months and hence the disgusting, rancid smell.

I was just delighted that it wasn't any of us, although there was a time where it was touch and go!

As for Hughie, he was never again asked to look after a school pet.

Well, if he was, he never cracked a light about it to me!

Fighting Fire with Fire!

...

In order to get results, sometimes certain cops would take matters into their own hands and deal out their own summary justice.

Such was the case one night when a silent alarm was activated at a village post office.

With all haste, officers attended at the location, arriving in silence in order not to alert the persons breaking in, and conscious of the fact that one of them was being a lookout on the post office roof.

As they approached on foot, under the cover of darkness and totally unnoticed by the lookout, they discovered an extending aluminium ladder at the rear of the building, leaning against the wall.

Quietly one of the cops, big Jimmy Doyle, climbed the ladder to the roof, where he saw the male lookout at the front of the building, armed with a metal shovel, looking up and down the street for any unwanted persons approaching.

He also noticed a large gaping hole on the roof, where they had burst through to gain entry into the post office.

Unseen by the suspect, Jimmy tiptoed up behind him, safely negotiating his way around the hole, and tapped him on the shoulder, frightening the life out of the suspect.

Jimmy then put his hand up to his lips and signalled him to keep quiet, before relieving him of the metal shovel he was armed with.

He then whispered, 'How many of your pals are inside the post office?'

The suspect whispered back, in a Liverpudlian accent, 'Just the two.'

'Just the two of them?' Jimmy enquired. 'Good! Are they armed with any weapons on them?'

'Why don't you ask them yourself?!' replied the suspect.

At which point Jimmy whispered, 'So you're not going to tell me?'

'No way. I've told you enough already!' he replied, getting louder as he spoke.

'OK, then,' said Jimmy, pointing towards some high-rise apartments in the distance. 'See that block of houses over there, all lit up?'

The suspect turned around to look where Jimmy was pointing.

'Yeah, what about them?' he asked with a certain amount of interest, when all of a sudden – CLANG! – followed by loud screams of excruciating PAIN! – followed by a really sickening THUD!

Jimmy had walloped him on the back of the head with the shovel, knocking him clean off the post office roof on to the concrete ground below, where he landed in a heap!

As a result of the squeals of pain heard coming from their accomplice, the others in the post office popped their heads out of the hole in the roof to check what was happening and were promptly confronted with Jimmy, standing over them, armed with the shovel.

'Don't tell me,' said Jimmy. 'Let me guess! You've an urgent giro you needed to cash and couldn't wait!'

Summary justice, expertly handed out by big Jimmy!

Blind Man's Bus

• • •

During a football detail, I was assigned to escort the football 'special supporters' buses, parked near to the stadium, on to the motorway to clear the area as quickly as possible.

As each bus filled with supporters, I would lead them on to the motorway and return for the next one.

However, after performing this task several times, I returned to a bus that was full up, but the driver was refusing to budge because the upstairs was totally over-crowded.

I boarded the bus and went upstairs and, to every double seat occupied by more than two passengers, I said, 'Off! Off! Off!'

As they went down the stairs to get off, some of them, rather than get off, forced their way into the downstairs compartment – 'Standing room only'.

Aware that this was taking place, I then went downstairs and grabbing hold of the supporters nearest the door, I again said, 'Off! Off! Off! Off!'

A respectably dressed passenger intervened and said, 'Excuse me, officer, but these passengers are all blind.'

Without any hesitation, I quickly grabbed hold of them by the collar and one by one said, 'On! On! On! On!'

Superglue the Locks

. . .

There used to be an arrogant shopkeeper who ran a licensed grocer shop next door to the police station where I worked.

The previous owner had been a very nice man who had a good relationship with the police in the area and refused to sell alcohol to anyone appearing to look underage – in fact, you had to look twenty-one or over.

He even refused to sell the likes of Buckfast tonic wine and some of the other cheaper designer drinks.

However, the new owner was in complete contrast and was prepared to sell to anybody.

He also, very early on in his occupancy of the shop, showed a total disregard for the police and displayed a blatant anti-police attitude.

This made him very popular with the local neds and very unpopular with the local parents. It also did nothing to enhance his relationship with us.

Within a very short time, the complaints arrived at the office in writing and by anonymous telephone calls, that many of the local underage neds were purchasing their 'Buckie' and cheap White Lightning cider from Warner's off-licence shop.

A call was made at Mr Warner's shop and he was made aware of the complaints we had received.

Mr Warner, who was a tall, arrogant and sarcastic character, denied selling the alcohol to any underage person, and if other people were buying alcohol on their behalf and supplying them with it, it was absolutely nothing to do with him.

He added that if he didn't sell it to them, they would go elsewhere, so he might as well get the business!

It was extremely annoying to learn that a shop-keeper such as Mr Warner was prepared to knowingly sell alcohol to an adult, aware that he was purchasing it for a minor.

Where were his morals and sense of responsibility, never mind his respect for the law?

Due to the ongoing complaints of vandalism and disturbances being caused by youths in the area drinking alcohol, we finally set up a watch on the shop to catch Mr Warner selling the alcohol.

Several hours had passed when a group of about five youths, aged between thirteen and sixteen, gathered outside the shop.

Moments later the tallest of them appeared to gather money from the others and entered the shop.

Within a short time, he came out the shop, minus any alcohol.

The youths loitered about outside the shop, approaching several adults as they entered and asking them to buy them alcohol.

The majority refused, but it only takes one and he came along shortly afterwards and, taking their money, he entered the shop, returning a very short time later laden down with two bottles of cheap wine, which he handed over to the youths immediately outside the front door of Mr Warner's shop and in full view.

The man was stopped and charged with selling and/or supplying alcohol to persons underage.

The youths had their names taken, were relieved of their alcohol and their parents were informed.

As for Mr Warner, his attitude was that if someone was buying alcohol and giving it to someone outside his premises, then that was nothing to do with him.

Charges against Mr Warner were dropped and smug Warner continued to trade and find ways of supplying cheap wine to the youths of the area.

However, as a final part of the story, the festive period was approaching and, like every other shopkeeper, Mr Warner was stocking up with alcohol for his busiest day of the year – Hogmanay. Yes, the day before the start of a new year when we all celebrate the end of an old year and the beginning of the next one with lots of booze!

You could hardly move in Warner's shop for boxes on boxes of the stuff, and he had also spent considerable time and effort making up posters to advertise his special alcohol bargains, and had tied them to lamp posts, railings and had even pasted them on walls around the area.

No matter where you looked there was a poster for 'Warner Off Sales'. They had sprung up everywhere overnight.

This prompted numerous complaints from the other shopkeepers in the area.

I decided to make a visit to Mr Warner and confront him.

Along with a colleague, I called at his shop and spoke with him regarding the fly bill posting, particularly immediately outside some of his competitors' shops, but Warner was a smug and arrogant big bastard with a total disregard for anyone else and he refused to listen, citing the festive period as his busiest time of the year and he was out to make a killing.

This total lack of compassion and respect for his fellow shopkeepers and his obvious arrogance towards me was disrespectful and I realised that there was no reasoning with Mr Warner.

Therefore there was no hiding the utter joy and delight from the other shopkeepers, and a wry smile of satisfaction from myself, when it was learned that on the morning of Hogmanay, 31 December, Mr Warner had arrived at eight in the morning with extra staff to open his premises for business, only to discover that someone had tampered with the locks of his security shutters and he was unable to open his shop.

Now guess who Mr Warner turned too, seeking assistance?

Yours truly!

Try as I might, I had difficulty getting a locksmith who was working that day and was free to attend.

When I eventually did manage to get one, the earliest he could come to try and repair it would be teatime, and for that he wanted paid double time with the money paid up front!

Reluctantly, a disgruntled Mr Warner agreed to this request.

Finally, in order to keep him and his extra staff occupied, I informed him that if he did not go down the main street and remove all those illegal bill posters from the railings, lamp posts and walls, I would charge him with littering and malicious mischief, rubbing more salt into his already deep wounds.

Frustrated and exasperated, Warner had his staff go around and remove all the bill posters.

I would hazard a guess that when Warner eventually gained entry to his premises at about 4.30 p.m. that day, he had a hard shift trying to make up for lost time and revenue, having given all his competitors a clear eight hours' head start.

Afterwards, I spoke with the locksmith and it would appear someone had squirted what he reckoned was superglue into the locks, causing Mr Warner's problem.

Who was responsible?

Well, Mr Warner made many enemies in a very short time – customers, parents, shopkeepers, etc – but I have my own suspicions . . .

'Evenin' all!'

Who Needs a Bus in Drumchapel

...

Thinking about growing up in a housing scheme in Drum-chapel reminded me of the things we used to do to entertain ourselves.

I remember having a metal-rimmed circular wheel, with a small round wheel joining it to a long metal rod. It was called a gird and cleek. It was fantastic and you would roll the larger metal rim while holding the rod and pushing it so that it rolled along the road.

Now this was the Rolls-Royce of girds, but an old bicycle wheel minus the spokes and a stick to hit it with was just as good. Even more so if it still had the white-wall tyre on it.

My mother would send me to the shops for a loaf of bread and I would take my gird with me. I would be off like a bullet from a gun, running like the clappers with my gird.

I would run from the Drum to Balloch and back, without a murmur, so long as I had my gird with me, and I did it in jig time.

Now my younger brother Hughie had an imaginary horse and, likewise, he could run like hell with this. I think it was white, although its colour would change daily because he had a few in his stable, if you know what I mean (headbanger!).

My dad would be craving a cigarette and send Hughie to the shops for a packet of five Woodbine.

Hughie would be about to leave on his horse and my dad would say, 'Take yer white horse, son, it's much faster than the rest!'

No sooner said and he was off, and the harder he slapped his arse, the faster he, or should I say his horse Silver, would run.

Lester Piggott would have been left in his slipstream.

Just as well there weren't any of today's social workers about in those days, or my mother would have had a lot of explaining to do about the welts on Hughie's bare arse from slapping his horse! It was red raw!

Ah, well, those were the days, and a long time before performance-enhancing drugs!

No Smoking

・・・

An old police sergeant walked into a hotel gift shop and bought a packet of cigarettes.

He opened the packet and, taking one out, lit it up.

As he puffed away, perusing the gifts on offer, the female assistant said, 'Excuse me, sir, but we don't allow smoking in the gift shop!'

The sergeant replied rather indignantly, 'Well, if you are going to sell me cigarettes in here, I think it is only right that I be allowed to smoke them in here!'

The assistant replied very calmly, 'That's true, sir, we do sell cigarettes to customers. But we also sell condoms in here as well. However, that doesn't mean if you buy them in here you're allowed to shag in the hotel foyer!'

Waterbed

. . .

From *The Adventures of Harry the Polis*

(Harry and Spook are in the front office of the station.)

HARRY: See my missus? I think her hormones are a bit dodgy!

SPOOK: What gives you dat idea, man?

HARRY: Well, she's never done reading those Mills and Boon books and she's started talking right dirty to me. Y'know – suggestive!

SPOOK: Is we talking dah romantic stuff here, den?

HARRY: Well, lately, when I come back from the pub and I've swallowed six or seven pints o' lager and gubbed a really hot Chic Murray, I'm just no' exactly in the mood!

SPOOK: I knows how ya feel, man!

HARRY: Now she's went and bought a waterbed to try and spice up our sex life.

SPOOK: And is it working?

HARRY: Naw! It's like the Dead Sea – we're just drifting apart!!

The Happy Clappy and the Whisky Chaser

· · ·

This story is not for the faint-hearted!

Prior to me taking up backshift duty one Sunday afternoon, my next door neighbour, who was a deep-sea diver, arrived at my house with a bucketful of fresh clappydoos, which to the uninitiated are very large sea molluscs with a dark elongated shell, similar to mussels only much, much bigger!

I decided to cook them and take them with me to work to share with my colleagues on the shift.

After cooking them, I just had to try one or two for myself.

They were absolutely delicious.

I then removed them from their shells and placed them into a large plastic Tupperware tub with the water they were cooked in and added some malt vinegar.

Once inside the police station, a few of my fellow officers tried them, but a few others were very sceptical and couldn't look at them, never mind eat one. I myself couldn't resist eating a few more.

As the day progressed, officers would call in to sample my cooked clappydoos, while others, who had never seen one before, would call in just to look at the size of them.

Near the end of my shift, big Archie came in and said he had a couple of bottles of whisky and would I like to join him and Beano for a few drams when we finished.

'Sure thing!' I said. 'And I'll bring the rest of my clappy-doos with me.'

'Aye, do that.'

After finishing our shift, we met up to have our drink and a feast of clappydoos.

What a concoction – seafood, in the shape of a large clappydoo, soaked in vinegar, all washed down with a large whisky chaser.

Totally disgusting, I know, but it seemed like a good idea at the time.

Big Archie was the first to get scunnered with the 'clappies'.

In fact, within a very short time he was boakin' at the thought of eating any more and he had only tried one!

Beano lasted a bit longer, however.

By the time we opened the second bottle of whisky, he had gave up on the clappies, leaving me to polish off the rest of them.

Now by this time, I wasn't even chewing them any more – I was stuffing the big clappydoo into my gub and like a Saltcoats seagull, I was swallowing it down whole, quickly followed by a large whisky chaser to help wash it down.

This continued for a short time until I had devoured the last of my clappies, and, along with big Archie and Beano, we had drunk three bottles of whisky between us.

With the bevvy now finished, we parted company.

I finally arrived home and went into the house, trying to keep as quiet as possible so as not to disturb the family.

As I leaned over to switch off a lamp that had been left on for me, I stumbled and struck one of my collection of decorative wall plates with my head, breaking it, which caused a chain reaction as the pieces struck other plates below them, knocking them off the wall and smashing them on the tiled floor below.

To prevent any further destruction, I made my way to my bed and, as quickly and quietly as possible, I got undressed and slipped into bed.

As I lay there, motionless, watching the bedroom ceiling spinning around before my eyes, I received a sudden jolt in my stomach. I looked down just in time to see it happen again.

This was certainly not normal. I felt like something alien was about to burst out of me, like what happened to John Hurt in *Alien*.

Whatever it was, it wanted out *right now*!

I decided it was best if I got up from my bed and went outside for some fresh air.

I went to the back garden and got my Alsatian from his kennel and went out the rear gate on to the nearby golf course for a walk! Well, actually, a stagger!

As I made my way up the course, three steps forward and two steps back, the *Alien* stomach action started up again, then – bbllurrpp! bang! – this perfectly shaped clappydoo, without as much as a tooth mark on it, came spurting out my mouth like a Scud missile, landing about five metres away on the perfectly cut golf course.

Several other missile births quickly followed this one in jig time, as I regurgitated the lot.

By the way, I never knew I could do this. Talented or what?

In my drunken state, looking down at them, they looked like miniature ETs, all perfectly shaped and forming a neat little trail along the golf course towards the green.

I half expected one to point at me and say, 'Phone home!'

I remember my dog looking at them, trying to work out what they were and getting such a fright he jumped back and landed in a sand bunker.

I had to use a sand wedge to get him back out.

He then looked over at me as if to say, 'What the hell have you been eating, big man?'

After walking for a short time around the course to clear my head and convince myself I was not going to give birth to any more clappies, I decided to make my way back to the house.

As for my dog, he was playing it safe and keeping his distance, just in case.

When I got back into bed, I slept like a newborn baby, farting in my underwear and snoring like a pig, thanks to the concoction of booze and seafood I had consumed earlier.

I could have peeled the paint off the walls with my breath.

However, when I woke later on that morning I had a light-hearted chuckle to myself over a cup of coffee when I thought about the golf course green-keeper, or a golfer on his morning round, discovering this trail of neatly formed sea mollusc aliens lining the course and wondering to themselves, how the hell did they managed to get there?

Now, that is what I call a conundrum!

Chap at the Door

• • •

Lately, since I left the police, I have been trying to modify my way of chapping or knocking on a door, for the following reason.

One night whilst on duty, I received a call to attend at a certain address.

I made my way there and on my arrival I knocked on the door, as I would do normally.

There was no immediate response, which prompted me to knock again, this time more loudly.

A female voice cried out, 'Yeah, yeah, yeah, I bloody heard you the first time!'

Moments later, the door was opened by a small, frail, grey-haired elderly woman who, on seeing me standing there in full uniform, said, 'Do you big bastards get taught to chap doors like that and deliberately frighten the life out of us old people?'

Answers from Real Police Scotland Exams

• • •

Real answers written down at the Police Scotland Exams:

'Serious assault is to assault someone to the infusion of blood'!

'Assault is when you strike someone using any part of your body'! (I suppose if you used your penis that would be considered an assault with a friendly weapon!)

Taxi for Troon

· · ·

One of the more enjoyable duties of the police was the Glasgow black hackney taxi annual outing to Troon, put on for disabled children.

The same taxi drivers that we all too often are quick to criticise would give up an entire working day to decorate their black cabs to look like cartoon characters, space-ships and castles, with balloons and the like covering every part of the bodywork.

Then they would call at various schools and collect their happy and excited young passengers.

Once all were aboard, we would congregate at Kelvin Way where the Lord Provost of Glasgow would say a few words before picking the best-decorated taxi.

After the formalities were completed, as part of the police motorcycle team we would begin the difficult but enjoyable task of escorting our very large, colourfully decorated convoy of taxis through the busy city centre streets, where the town workers would be standing outside their shops and waving from the windows of the office blocks.

The taxi drivers and other motorists would all be sounding their car horns and their young passengers would be lapping it all up and vigorously waving back at everyone.

Like an army going into battle, we would snake our way down through the city centre, keeping them all together as one, passing through sets of traffic lights, with the police motorcycle outriders holding up the traffic in order to

keep the colourful convoy flowing freely and uninterrupted.

This would continue all the way through Shawlands
Cross and out the Fenwick Road, on our way to the A77
taking us to Ayrshire and our final destination for the day,
Troon.

However, the first time I took part in escorting the taxi
outing, I called at my allotted school, where the decorated
taxis were already in attendance.

As I parked and waited outside for the drivers and their
passengers to fill their cabs, a smart, casually dressed
young man approached me.

'How's it hanging, big man? Are you looking forward to
the big day?' he asked me.

'Definitely,' I replied enthusiastically. 'It looks like being
a good one and the weather forecast is meant to be sunny
and warm as well,' I added.

'Yeah, it's usually a great day for everybody,' he
responded.

As he stood there in front of me making idle conversation, I said, 'So what taxi is yours, then?'

He turned around and pointed at a taxi decorated like
the Eiffel Tower.

'I'm in that one there,' he replied, pointing casually
towards it.

'It looks brilliant!' I said. 'You must be in with a shout
for the best-decorated-taxi prize?'

'Well, I hope so – I like winning!'

As we waited for the other drivers and kids to come out
from the school, he said to me, 'I think I'll join the police.'

'Oh, aye? Have you been considering it?' I asked him, trying to appear interested.

'Yeah,' he replied. He then took a step closer to me and pointed to the badge on my breast pocket and said, 'I know what that says.'

He then pointed to the letters one at a time and said, 'B-U-R . . .' He then paused for a moment before continuing, '. . . T-R-S – Police,' delighted with himself.

As I sat on my police motorcycle looking at him, trying to work it out if he was yanking my chain, a well-dressed young lady appeared from the doorway of the school.

'David Ritchie!' she called out with a voice of authority. 'I've been looking everywhere for you! Sorry about that, officer, he talks to everybody,' she said.

As she walked over and took hold of his hand and led him back inside, she asked, 'How many times have you been told not to go wandering?'

As for me, my face must have been a picture to behold. I had automatically assumed my passengers would all be small children, but no.

It turned out that David Ritchie was a mature pupil with learning disabilities.

So it just goes to show you that David, with his learning disability, had totally duped me and for a short time he had me believing that he was my friend and one of the taxi drivers, when in fact, he was one of the rear-seat passengers on an away day with the taxi outing to Troon!

Ear, Nose and Bum

· · ·

It is amazing the effect that a police vehicle in the rear-view mirror can have on the average car driver.

One minute they're driving along, quite the thing, with other things on their mind, then suddenly they look up and guess who is right behind them? The polis!

Most car drivers' immediate response is to look at their dashboard to check their speed, then they begin the erratic fidgeting before putting their hand up to their face and rubbing it vigorously.

The forefinger then nervously begins to explore all facial orifices, ending with two fingers lodged up both nostrils to the bridge. They then travel through the sinus passage to perform some brain surgery while up there.

From this position, the said finger finds its way back around to the ear and a good poking of the ear wax takes place, with a right good shaking of the finger and head simultaneously.

A thorough self-examination has taken place without the presence of a qualified doctor.

If you don't believe me, then just check out your own reaction the next time you're driving and check your rear-view mirror to see the police following close behind you.

Mind you, that's not as bad as the ones who would physically shit themselves.

You'll know who *you* are!

Exposed

...

From *The Adventures of Harry the Polis*

(Harry and Orville are in the front office.)

HARRY: I hear old Phil MacCracken was up in court today.

ORVILLE: What was it for this time?

HARRY: It seems he was exposing himself and flashing his boaby in public again.

ORVILLE: Crikey! He must be about sixty-three years old. How did he get on?

HARRY: The judge sentenced him to a year probation.

ORVILLE: Is it no' about time he called it a day and retired?

HARRY: Well, apparently he was going to, but now he's decided to stick it out for another couple of years!

Answers from Real Police Scotland Exams

...

Definition of the common law crime of assault and threats is:

'Assault: any direction taken by another to another.'

'Threats: to threaten someone verbally or by use of the telephone.'

The Greedy Dog

...

It used to be that, during the old City of Glasgow Police days, prior to amalgamation to form Strathclyde Police, we had really unsociable shifts.

One particular tour of duty was a five-week nightshift. This would consist of seven days on and two off, seven on and two off, etc, for the complete five-week tour.

During the early days of my police service I lived in Renfrew and, in order to get to my work, I had to leave the house at 7.30 p.m. to start at 9 p.m., finishing at seven the following morning and arriving back home at about 8.45 a.m.

As you will appreciate, I would be extremely tired and looking forward to getting into bed and enjoying a good undisturbed sleep.

Directly below me in the tenement block lived a woman called Ella who owned a pet terrier, whom she doted on and treated like the baby she never had.

However, she worked daily in an office and subsequently left her dog in the house all day. As a result, a constant barrage of barking from the lonely dog would greet any person visiting the tenement close.

Subsequently, my sleep would be regularly interrupted, several times a day!

About three weeks into my nightshift tour, I was becoming frustrated and agitated with the continual barking mad interruptions to my much-needed sleep and had occasion to speak with Jim, the next door neighbour.

Jim was a fireman and had endured this unsociable

behaviour from her for over two years. He informed me that he had complained to her about the noise of her dog on numerous occasions, but she declined to discuss the matter with him, saying he could sleep during his watch!

Also, on another occasion, the dog had bitten his infant daughter and Ella had responded by saying that his young daughter had hit the dog, prompting this reaction by it.

Finally enough was enough and I decided it was time for me to speak to Ella about her dog and his non-stop daily barking and yelping!

One evening I called at her door and politely informed her of my dilemma with regards to her dog continually disrupting my sleep, but to no avail.

Ella was very rude towards me and somewhat dismissive of my plea to find a solution.

She just didn't want to know and interrupted me repeatedly to make the point that her medium-sized terrier called Max was not just a family pet but a watchdog, and he was doing exactly what was required of him and totally what was expected by her when he was left alone in the house.

She also suggested that Jim and I were conspiring against her and her pet!

With no amicable solution being considered by Ella, it was left to me to find an answer to my problem, that is, if I wanted to enjoy a normal uninterrupted sleep.

Next morning, I called at the local chemist's shop and purchased two bars of laxative chocolate and returned to my tenement building.

As I climbed the stairs, Max began barking and the closer I got to Ella's stair landing, the louder he became, until I was standing outside her front door.

Max was going mad inside and was also scratching at her door.

I quickly unwrapped a bar of the chocolate and posted it through the letter box.

The response was immediate, as the barking stopped and I could hear Max munching away noisily on the chocolate.

'Do you like that, Max?' I asked.

Quickly unwrapping the second bar of chocolate, I said, 'Here you go, then, cop for that!' pushing the second bar through the letter box.

The greedy bugger could hardly wait for it to land on the floor and almost snatched it from my hand as I posted it through.

The noises from inside were incredible – munchety-munchety, slabber-slabber!

Convinced that Max had devoured both bars without a trace, I left him to enjoy the inevitable reaction – the loosening of the bowels!

Next morning I followed the same procedure and purchased another two bars of chocolate laxative and, just like the previous day, Max heralded my arrival on the stairway by barking and growling at the door.

Again the reaction was immediate from Max, as I posted the chocolate bars through the letter box – munchety-munchety, slabber-slabber!

This became my daily ritual for Max over the next few

weeks, even on my days off. He just couldn't resist his chocolate treat, no matter what!

The wee soul – I think he looked forward to it! Bless him!

Then one morning I was late arriving home and had unwrapped the chocolate, ready to feed him, when Ella and Max met me on the stairway.

Max was a shadow of his old self with clapped-in jaws. What a difference a few weeks make – he had reduced in size to that of a Yorkshire terrier and, although he was obviously showing signs of excessive weight loss, the little bugger could smell his chocolate laxative treat in my coat pocket and was jumping up, sniffing and trying to retrieve what was now his daily fix!

Ella, for her part, explained that he had been very unwell and had lost complete control of his bowels and had fouled the house regularly over the past few weeks.

She was convinced it was a virus of some sort and was taking the day off work to visit the vet to have him thoroughly examined.

However, with Max continuing to try and get into my pockets, I made my excuses and left her to get on with it, while I made a hasty retreat.

Max had to be restrained by Ella as he desperately tried to go with me.

Thinking back, if I had been arriving home at my usual time, Ella would have caught me feeding Max his treat through the letter box!

As it was, Ella was to make several visits to the vet with Max as I kept up his chocolate laxative diet.

On another occasion, I was passing her door and Ella opened it to greet me, along with a rather subdued Max (the cat had got his tongue, maybe)!

'Could you help me, Harry, and carry an old rug down to the bin area for me?' she asked. 'Max has ruined it. Poor wee soul – he just can't control his bowels!'

'No problem, Ella,' I replied as I entered her house.

'Whoah!' The house was minging. It smelt worse than the local abattoir and that was saying something.

Ella noticed me putting my hand up towards my face and about to nip my nose.

'You'll have to excuse the smell, Harry. Max has been so unwell. You'd think he was taking Andrews salts, the way it's pouring out of him!' Ella explained apologetically.

I thought to myself, 'Andrews salts? More like somersaults!' There were shit marks everywhere, even on the walls, and the carpet had a stain that resembled the map of the Ponderosa! (Remember the Cartwrights?)

While all this was going on, miniature Max (my new best pal) was sniffing around me like a dog in heat, sniffing out the unwrapped chocolate in my pocket.

'He really likes you, Harry!' Ella remarked. 'That's unusual – he usually doesn't like men at all!'

I quickly grabbed hold of the soiled rug that Ella had neatly rolled up and got out fast before I puked with the stench emanating from the room.

Within a few weeks, Max had been diagnosed by the vet as having what appeared to him as the human form of anorexia. Poor Max was trying to crap even when there was nothing left to crap.

His bomb doors, as they say, were permanently jammed open.

Ella tried taking him to another vet for a second opinion, but he too was baffled as to the dog's rapid weight loss and basically didn't have a clue!

Suffice to say if there had been a Weight Watchers' Slimmer of the Year award for animals, Max would have won it paws down!

With no obvious cure available, Max withered away to nothing and eventually died peacefully in his sleep (poor wee soul!).

A fitting epitaph would be: 'The chocolate lax was the death of Max'! Or 'Death by chocolate'!

What a pleasant nightshift tour I had when it came around again – it was tranquil.

Mind you! It was too bloody tranquil and it took me a few weeks to get used to the complete silence of not having mad Max around barking.

However, a week or two AMD (after Max death), I was in the local chemist's shop and the pharmacist enquired with genuine sincerity and concern if my bowel problem had been resolved!

How thoughtful!

The Special Olympics

• • •

Out one night on patrol in Castlemilk, I was assigned a young special constable called Steven – 'Call me Stevie' – to accompany me while my regular colleague cleared up some urgent paperwork at the office.

A special constable was a male or female civilian who had a real day job and wanted to experience what it was like to work as a police officer, and gave up their precious time to patrol a particular area with a real policeman.

This was of great assistance to a stretched and under-manned police force such as Glasgow.

They would be issued with a full uniform and, while working alongside a regular police officer, they held the rank of constable and were entitled to enforce the duties and powers associated with that title, all for a considerably small amount of pay – usually a paltry sum and expenses only!

Not every cop liked working with one and felt they prevented them from getting overtime, due to their presence, and, as they would say, 'You wouldn't like it if I came to your work and did the same job as you for the equivalent of two bob, a hat and a balloon!'

I'm rambling on, but that describes a special, so back to the story.

We were out in the panda when we were flagged down by a man waving frantically in the middle of the road.

'Quick, officer!' he said excitedly. 'Some wee bastard has just blagged my motor from the roadway right outside my house!'

I pulled over to the side of the road, whereby the man

got into the back seat and I noted the make and model of his stolen car. Once I had all the details I was in the process of relaying them over the radio to my station controller for him to broadcast over the air to other mobile stations, when all of a sudden the male screamed out, 'There it's! That's my motor! The bastard's driving my motor!'

As I looked up, I saw the stolen Ford Capri coming towards us on the opposite side of the road, with a young man driving it.

I immediately performed a U-turn and gave chase, trying to concentrate on my driving while my frantic passenger screamed hysterically in my ear, 'Get him! Get him! Get the wee bastard! If he's damaged my motor he's dead! Look at the paintwork – it's gleaming!'

As I closed up on the stolen car, it began to slow down and the driver's door opened. Next thing, the driver put his legs out the car on to the road and started to run alongside it.

Eventually pulling his whole body out while holding on to the door, he then let go of the car and ran off in the opposite direction.

I pulled up and stopped, allowing my young 'special' companion Stevie to get out and give chase after the suspect. Keen as mustard, this boy!

In the meantime, the stolen car, now minus a driver, was still careering along the dual carriageway out of control, with the driver's door wide open. Now, if it went to the right, it would've hit the kerb and rolled on to the central reservation before coming to a stop, but, unfortunately for the owner of the stolen car, it veered left and collided with the only other thing in sight – a big yellow Corporation bus shelter.

Watching this entire episode happening, in what could only be described as like slow motion, and physically unable to do anything to prevent it, the frantic owner by now was screaming obscenities in the rear of the panda.

'Ya bastard! Ya rotten wee bastard! I'll rip yer bastarding head off when I get ye!'

Then, as his car collided with the bus shelter, he shouted, 'Naw! Naw! Naw! No' my baby!' Then, 'Aw, ya bastard! My motor! That's it – he's dead, he's fuckin' dead!'

All the while he had his hands on my shoulders and was digging his nails into me, which prompted me to have to tell him, 'Cool the beans, sir, you're hurting me!' (The polite version!)

Meanwhile, Special Constable Stevie was hard on the heels of our suspect, who had run through the front of a tenement close into the back courts, which were in total darkness.

Wallop! Snap! Whoosh! Bang! Thud!

'Oh, ya bastard!' was the cry.

Poor Stevie had forgotten about the dangers of tenants leaving up their clothes lines and had run smack into one, which caught him round about his neck and spun him up and around like a peerie.

I believe he did two triple somersaults, a backward double twist, followed by a half-pike before landing spectacularly on his napper.

On an Olympic scorecard, he would score the equivalent of four nines and a straight ten and be in the silver medal position.

Not bad for someone who didn't train to do gymnastics.

Olga Korbut no doubt would have been impressed.

However, while Stevie was performing these moves and letting the suspect get away, as he thought, I followed him through the same tenement close, in anticipation of assisting him with the arrest of the suspect.

Being slightly wiser and having been caught out before by the clothes-line dangers of a dark back court myself, I stopped at the back entrance in order to survey the area and allow my eyes to adjust to the darkness.

While looking for some movement, I saw a silhouette of Stevie struggling to get to his feet and called out to him, 'Is that you, Stevie? Are you all right?'

'I think so!' he replied. 'But I lost our suspect – he just disappeared. Don't know where he went!'

He had only just uttered these words when suddenly I was struck on the shoulder by a small roughcast pebble from the wall above me.

As I looked up, I saw the figure of our suspect hanging out of the stair landing window above, but he hadn't seen me below.

I tiptoed upstairs and, as I neared the window, I saw him hanging on to the window ledge by his fingertips like grim death.

So I surprised him by jumping in front of the window and shouting as loud as I could, 'Boo!'

The suspect got such a fright, he lost his grip and fell from the window ledge, landing with a thump on the paving slabs below.

Unfortunately for him, he broke his ankle in the fall and had to be conveyed to hospital afterwards.

The expression on the face of the officer on duty at the police station had to be seen, for after the suspect was charged with the offences, he was asked how he had injured himself and he said rather pathetically, 'That big polis did it! He shouted "Boo!" at me and gave me such a fright I lost my grip o' the windae ledge and fell aff!'

Boo! Ya wee wimp!

However, it's just a pity that 'Boo!' doesn't work more often!!

Thomas Who?

. . .

I called into an office one day trying to trace a man whom I only knew as Thomas.

'Can I help you, officer?' asked the girl in reception.

'I hope so,' I replied. 'I'm trying to trace an office worker employed here called Thomas.'

'Thomas who?' asked the receptionist. 'And what department?'

'I don't know,' I replied, shrugging my shoulders.

The young girl then turned around to an older woman several desks away and called out, 'Mary, do you know a Thomas who works here?'

To which the woman asked, 'Thomas who?'

The young receptionist replied excitedly, 'That's him – Thomas Who! What department does he work in?'

Choir Practice in the Morning

. . .

Many a night, long-suffering partners would have their homes invaded by police colleagues brought back for a bit of 'choir practice' (a drinking binge!) at the end of a long and arduous shift.

Such was the case one particular morning, off the night-shift at 7 a.m., when someone, probably myself, came up with an excuse for a drinking session and another cop offered up his house as the venue.

As we arrived en masse at his house, we filtered in one by one through the patio doors so as not to disturb his sleeping family at the opposite end of the house.

Whisky, vodka and several cans of beer were opened and quickly drunk, during which bucketloads of utter pish were spouted by just about everyone present, yours truly included.

It wasn't long before there was a queue longer than a signing-on line at the burroo, all along the hallway outside his toilet.

'Harry, Harry,' said Beano, 'I'm really bursting, man! Honest, I'm desperate! If I don't go now I'll do it in my trousers!'

'Why don't you go outside into his garden and do it?'

'There's no way I'm going outside. I couldn't do that!' he said.

'Quick, then,' I suggested. 'Use his kitchen sink, and hurry up about it while I watch the door for you.'

'Oh, thanks, Harry. I owe you one!' he said.

While standing there looking out for him, I thought about what he had just said – 'I owe you one'?

Owe me one what? A pish?! I don't think so!

Just at that, my thoughts were interrupted when Beano called out to me, 'Harry! Any chance you could get me some toilet paper?'

As I turned around, all I saw was Beano with his trousers at his ankles and legs dangling, with his bare arse in the kitchen sink!

Mind you, he did have the manners to empty the sink of all dishes first.

Now that's what I call a good upbringing!

Answers from Real Police Scotland Exams

• • •

'Incest (defence) – they were in a healthy state of mind when the act took place.' *Don't think so!*

Englishman in Moscow

· · ·

A quick story about using decorum and common sense at all times is the one about the traditional Scottish folk band I used to manage and perform with, while we were on tour in Moscow in winter 1999.

When we arrived in Russia we were driven to our hotel, the Grand Marriott, right in the centre of Moscow, and after checking in we were taken to the Central House of Journalists for a press conference.

It was all very exciting, with over a hundred journalists awaiting our arrival.

We were seated at a top table with two beautiful young female interpreters to translate the questions and our responses.

Afterwards, we were scheduled to give a concert in the large hall within the Central House building.

We returned later that evening to a full house of journalists and invited guests and received an encouraging welcome from our enthusiastic audience, as we took to the stage in our colourful tartan kilts and feileadh-mhors.

After a few well-known Scottish songs, which were well received by our new friends, Ian, the lead vocalist, asked the audience, 'Are there any Englishmen in the hall tonight?'

One man, about halfway up the hall, put his hand up. At which point Ian said (jokingly, of course!), 'Get out!'

The band then went straight into our next song, 'Killiecrankie', during which a very large Russian man, built like a brick shithouse, got up from his seat, walked over to where the Englishman was sitting, picked him up by the neck and promptly punched him full in the face.

Or as we say in Glasgow, he gave him a dull yin!

For a moment or two afterwards, there was a bit of a stramash as both men threw several punches before peace was restored and they returned to being allies.

When we finished the song, I made reference to the disturbance, thanking them for making us feel like we were back home in Glasgow.

We then carried on with the rest of the show.

After the concert, I made a point of telling Ian and the rest of the band members, 'No more remarks during a concert about Englishmen, jokingly or not!' Our Russian agent had informed me that some of our vodka-swilling audiences had taken a dislike to our English neighbours, after seeing Mel Gibson's film *Braveheart*, which just happened to be on release in cinemas around Moscow at the time.

However, we did have a good laugh later that evening when we heard that the English victim in all of this turned out to be an Italian waiter. He had thought Ian had asked, 'Is there anyone who speaks English in the hall tonight?'

Big mistake!

With a bruised nose and black eye for his troubles, I would suggest he speako it notto very wello and understando it even lesso!

Comrade!

Talking Piss or Just Taking the Piss

...

It was a cold, cold nightshift and 'Soapy' and I were out patrolling our beat in the Oatlands area of Glasgow.

We had checked some of our shop premises and then, about 1.30 a.m., we went along to a local twenty-four-hours burger van for a hot roll and a cup of coffee to warm us up.

Soapy, as usual, complemented his coffee with a tot of brandy.

'Purely for medicinal purposes only, son!' he would say to me. 'My blood's not as thick as it used to be. Know what I mean, Harry boy?'

He would then tap the side of his nose with his fore-finger.

After Soapy thinned his blood down, we would return to our nightshift duties, checking the properties in our area.

About another hour had passed and we were outside a licensed premises called the Little Mill Vaults.

I went through to the rear to check the back door and when I returned to the front Soapy was standing beside one of our divisional CID cars, at the passenger door, talking to the occupants.

I approached them and, like all new young police officers, kept quiet and listened intently to their conversation, speaking only when asked for my opinion.

Whilst this was taking place, I suddenly heard a noise which clearly sounded like running water.

I went over to the Mill Vaults premises and shone my

torch in the window to check it, while Soapy remained standing at the CID car, chatting away to our colleagues with his arms on the roof of the car.

No obvious sign of water running in the pub, I looked back over to Soapy and could hardly believe my eyes as I saw where the water was running from.

Soapy was standing casually with both his arms resting on the CID car roof, chatting away to the car's occupants, while nonchalantly urinating out through the bottom of his police raincoat.

Now I'm not saying he was well endowed and hanging down below his raincoat, because he wasn't, but he obviously had a good aim and had perfected this disgusting behaviour over many years, because there wasn't even a drop, or should I say a drip, visible on his police-issue raincoat.

However, I was more amazed at the CID officers who must have heard him doing this and never even batted an eyelid as they carried on their conversation with Soapy, whilst he was in full flow!

Cosmetic Surgery Without the Op

...

Out one day with the missus, we were shopping at Parkhead Forge in Glasgow.

As I was walking around, I saw a banner with pictures of Princess Diana and Sir Cliff Richard on it. Curious to see what it said, I stepped over the roped-off area for a closer look.

It was an advert for 'cosmetic (facial) enhancement', claiming to take away your wrinkles (and laughter lines) with no need to go under the knife for a proper surgical operation.

I was just finishing reading the poster when a security guard, in all innocence, approached, looked me straight in the face and said, 'If you want to hold on, mate, she should be back in about ten minutes and she'll see to you then!'

I looked at the poster then back at the security guard.

As it sunk in what he had just said to me, I replied rather indignantly, 'What are you on about? Do I look like I need cosmetic surgery? Ya cheeky bastard!'

The poor security guard, trying to be helpful, didn't know where to look and did the next best thing and walked off, shaking his head!

As for my missus, she looked like the Joker from *Batman*, and it would have taken more than cosmetic surgery to wipe the permanent smile off her face!

Barry Manilow

· · ·

Big Brian Toner was a former colleague of mine who lived all of his life in the same house he was born in, over at Lesmahagow in South Lanarkshire.

Brian never got married until quite late into his thirties, when he met and eventually tied the knot with Maggie.

Being well known in the area, Brian was in the local butcher's shop in the main street and the butcher was congratulating him on his recent marriage.

'So where is she today, then, Brian, that you've got to do all the shopping?'

'Oh, Maggie's working today, but she has been in the shop before. In fact, you've served her personally!' said Brian.

'Have I?' enquired the butcher. 'What does she look like?'

Brian paused for a moment, then said, 'Put it this way – she looks like Barry Manilow wi' big tits!'

Later that day, Brian was telling his new wife Maggie about his conversation with the butcher and how he had described her to him.

Maggie listened intently, then said to Brian, 'Is that right? Well, see if I go into that butcher shop and he says, "Hello, Mrs Toner!" *you are dead*!'

The Glesca Polis Song

...

This is a poem/song told to me thirty-three years ago by my room-mate at Tulliallan Police College, who is now a deputy chief constable.

I have absolutely no idea where it comes from or who wrote it, but it is very Glaswegian, as the dialect shows.

The Thirty-Seven Bus

As I was oan the upper deck o' a thirty-seven bus
Ah saw big Jimmy swallowin' wine and kicking up a fuss.
The driver stoaped the bus right sherp and derted up the ster:
'Ye can get tae hell right aff ma bus if ye gimme any mer!'

'Aw, nae offence, pal,' big Jimmy said. 'If ye kent wit I'd been thru,
Ye widnae say such things tae me or blame a man that's foo.
I've lost a pile oan the dogs tonight, I'd huv ye for to know —
Aw ma wages doon the stank oan a dug that widnae go.'

The driver said he couldnae gie a monkey's or gie a tinker's cuss:
'Your shouting and yer swearing is distressing aw my bus.
Ah've had aboot enough o' you, a lot more than I need.
If you don't hawd that big tongue o' yours I'll stuff it doon yer heid.'

Well, Jimmy smiled and he picked his nose and he finished aff his wine.
He said, 'The way you spoke tae me has went right oot o' line.
I've finished aff fifteen o' youse, tae get intae a fight.
Get doon oan yer knees and pray for help, ya cheeky little shite!'

Well, the bus was in an uproar as the punters got aff right fast —
The good auld Glesca chivalry of woman and children last.
They shouted fur the driver 'cause they didnae like big Jim:
'C'mon, driver, sink the boot! Get tore right intae him!'

The driver waded intae Jim, a-swinging and kicking blows,
And finally caught big Jim's square heid a dull yin oan the nose.
Jim's knee came up, his fist came doon, and the driver moved nae mer
So he jumped a couple o' times oan his heid as he twitched upon the fler.

At this one hundred polis men were sent oot to capture Jim.
In twos and threes and dozens, he laid them oot roun' him,
But finally they captured him when the army sent a tank
But I coonted forty polis hats a-floatin' doon the stank.

Noo there's a notice oan the upper deck o' a thirty-seven bus:
'If ye see big Jimmy swallowin' wine or kicking up a fuss,
Don't try tae act the hero and put big Jimmy aff
'Cause the poor auld Glesca Polis Force jist cannae afford the staff.'

(Arrangement by Harry Morris)

Television is Much Better

. . .

Whilst out on patrol one day in an unmarked police car, two of my former colleagues stopped a driver for speeding, using the video surveillance equipment fitted to the police car.

After they had charged the driver, they explained that the surveillance video footage could be made available to him if he wished to contest the speeding charge in court.

He was then asked if he would like a copy of the video.

To which the driver replied, rather dejectedly,

'No thanks, mate. I think I'll just wait until it comes on the TV!'

Cannae Even Say It Right

. . .

When Wee Jock (the Yorkie) was working for the polis dog branch, he was assigned to the Mountain Rescue Team, to work alongside this big Alsatian called Alfie, trying to trace some hillwalkers who had failed to return from the snow-covered hills.

While trudging their way through the very cold, very thick snow, eight inches deep, Wee Jock, with his short four-inch legs, muttered, 'My fffrigging pppaws are ff-frozen!'

To which big Alfie replied, 'Aye! And yer speech is a bit slurred as well!'

Guess My Age?

• • •

This is one of those stories you hear over the years that you just have to include for posterity, if nothing else.

Old Tom, an elderly retired cop, was fed up looking in the mirror every morning at the heavy lines and drooping skin on his ageing face. So one day, whilst reading an article on cosmetic surgery, he decided to withdraw some of his hard-earned savings from his bank account and do something about it.

He rang the number in the advert and made an appointment to see a specialist consultant regarding some facial surgery.

After the consultation with the cosmetic surgeon, and his assurances of what he could do for him and the promise that he would look much younger afterwards, Tom decided, 'What the hell!' and booked up with the surgeon to go ahead and have it done.

Several weeks later, after the superficial scarring from his surgery had disappeared, old Tom – sorry, 'young' Tom – decided it was time to 'face' the outside world.

Dressed to kill and looking very dapper in his best suit, collar and tie, Tom made his way down to the main street, stopping off at the local newsagent's.

'I'll have a *Daily Record* please, Martha,' he said to the counter assistant.

The counter assistant looked at him as she handed over the paper and said, 'I'm terribly sorry sir, but do I know you?'

'Of course you do, Martha. It's *me* – Tom Boyd!' he replied.

'Good God, Tommy Boyd!' she remarked. 'I didn't recognise you. You look fantastic! In fact, you look about forty years of age!'

A very proud Tom responded, 'Well, I'm actually sixty-seven years old!'

'That's incredible, Tom, you're looking absolutely amazing!' she said.

After some further small talk, Tom left to continue his shopping.

As he walked along past the shops, he stopped off and entered a rather busy butcher's shop.

While standing in the queue, he couldn't resist tapping the shoulder of the woman in front of him and asking her, 'Excuse me, hen, but what age do you think I am?'

The woman looked Tom up and down before commenting, 'Ye're about forty-six!' she replied confidently.

This prompted Tom to ask the butcher to have a guess.

'I'd say you're between forty-two and forty-five years of age!' said the butcher.

Smiling and totally delighted with the results, Tom replied, 'Well, ye're both wrong. I'm sixty-seven years old!'

The people in the butcher's shop were amazed at his looks and there were several 'oohs' and 'aahs'.

After being served, Tom left the butcher's and walked over to the bus stop to wait for a bus to take him into the city centre.

Completely ecstatic about the response his new look was receiving, Tom decided to ask the only other person in the bus shelter, an elderly woman, 'Excuse me, missus, but do you mind if I ask you a personal question?'

'Not at all, son,' she replied.

'How old do you think I am?' he asked.

The elderly woman, looking intently, paused for a moment then said, 'I'm not really sure. I'd need to feel yer boaby to be able to tell ye exactly!' she replied.

'Feel my boaby? D'you mean my penis?' responded a surprised Tom.

'Aye, yer boaby! Penis! Tadger! Whitever ye want tae call it,' said the old woman. 'That is if ye have one and ye want me to guess yer age exactly right!'

Confident he could pass this unusual request, Tom said, 'Right, then, you're on!'

Tom slipped his zip down and the elderly woman put her hand through the opening in his underpants and grabbing hold of his penis.

She then fondled and rolled it around in her hand, having a right old grope at it, before taking her hand back out of his trousers.

'I'm no' very sure!' she said. 'I'd need to feel yer testes!'

'My testes?' enquired Tom. 'What's my testes?'

Quick as a flash, the elderly woman said, 'Aye, yer testes! You know, yer bollocks! The place where aw you men keep a nursery full of potential screaming weans! Mind you, that is if you want me tae guess yer age exactly right!'

Tom thought for a moment, then relented. 'OK, then, have a feel at my testes if you think it will help you guess my age exactly right!'

The elderly woman performed the same procedure, this time grabbing his bollocks and rolling them around in the palm of her hand like Humphrey Bogart's stress balls in

The Cain Mutiny. After several minutes she withdrew her hand.

At this, Tom zipped up his fly before composing himself and asking her, 'Well? What's your guess, then? How old am I?'

There was a slight moment's pause before the elderly woman blurted out, with complete confidence, 'Ye're exactly sixty-seven years old, ya silly auld bugger!'

Tom was totally stunned and shocked by this reply. 'How the hell did you know that?' he asked her.

'Dead easy,' replied the old woman. 'I was in the queue at the butcher's!'

Missing for Dinner
. . .

A woman called at the police station one night concerned about her husband, who had left the house the previous day to go to the shops for a tin of baked beans to go with the evening meal of pie and chips, and had since failed to return home.

'What should I do?' she asked me, distressed and desperately seeking an answer.

I paused for a moment, before responding, 'Just open a can of peas!'

Curl Up and Dye

• • •

From *The Adventures of Harry the Polis*

(Harry the Polis has dyed his hair and is going into the police station for the first time, but the guys on his shift already know.)

ORVILLE: Quick, here he comes! Everybody act normal.

(Harry walks into the office all nonchalant.)

HARRY: Good morning, everybody.
ORVILLE & SPOOK: Morning, Harry.
HARRY: D'you notice anything different aboot me?
ORVILLE: Nope. D'you notice anything, Spook?
SPOOK: I don't see nuttin' different, man!
HARRY: Are ye sure? Take a right good look at me.
ORVILLE: Oh, I see it now – you're growing a moustache! Very smart, Harry. You'll suit it.
HARRY: No! No! No! It's my hair. My hair's dyed!
ORVILLE: I hate to tell you this, Harry, but your hair died a long, long time ago!

Drug Dealers Dealt With

• • •

A drug case that I was involved with at the High Court in Glasgow involved four accused charged with possession and supply of a class A drug, namely heroin!

A deal was agreed by the advocate depute and the defence agents that two of the accused would plead not guilty and the Crown would accept this, and the remaining two would plead guilty and be sentenced by the court accordingly.

Also, the judge would be asked to take into account the fact that the accused were ready to accept the sentence imposed on them by the court without the expense of a court trial or the inconvenience caused to a jury and the numerous police witnesses.

Now, the following was overheard behind the scenes in the cell area.

The two main culprits in the drug case would be the ones to plead not guilty, and the two who played a lesser role would take the blame and plead guilty, thereby expecting to receive a shorter sentence than the main culprits and, as a reward, the two main culprits would look after their families with monetary payments and do likewise to them on their release from prison.

Expected prison term at worst? Two, maybe three years at most!

Back to the court case, and the pleas were put forward and, as agreed, they were accepted by the Crown.

However, the two accused pleading guilty were advised by their defence agent to put forward a motion (or excuse) to have their sentencing put back until the following day.

The thinking behind this was that, the following morning, the guilty pleas would be heard by a sheriff, performing the duties of a judge presiding over a High Court case, who was considered to be very lenient in his sentencing. Also, one of the defence QCs had an urgent engagement and did not wish to be delayed any further.

Unfortunately for them, on the Friday morning when they were to be sentenced, the said sheriff was taken ill and therefore was unavailable.

Subsequently, a judge had to be summoned from Edinburgh High Court, to be driven through to Glasgow to hear the pleas of the accused.

It's a known fact that all of our High Court judges prefer to be going in the opposite direction, i.e. Glasgow to Edinburgh, so they finish off in Edinburgh on a Friday, so the judge assigned to travel through to Glasgow would not be entirely happy about having to make the reverse journey.

Now, of the two accused remaining, one was a haulage contractor who had allowed one of his vehicles to be used in the transportation of the drugs, and the other was an elderly man who was basically a small-time dealer who had been concealing the drugs for the main players.

His Lordship took his seat on the bench and heard one defence agent plead for leniency on behalf of his client, the haulage contractor who had embroiled his family business in this illegal operation.

It was then the turn of the other defence agent, who began pleading the case for leniency on behalf of the elderly dealer.

He stated that his client was a fifty-seven-year-old male who was married and had watched his only son die recently from drug abuse, and that his client's own part in this entire episode was that of a 'small cog in a big wheel'!

'Stop right there!' the judge told the defence agent. 'I'm going to call for a ten-minute adjournment to allow you time to talk with your client and obtain for me the names and addresses of these "big wheels" involved in this entire episode and with whom he was associated!'

At that, the judge called for the adjournment.

Ten minutes later, the court was reconvened and the judge immediately called the defence agent and asked him if he had anything to tell him with regards to his request.

The defence agent said he reluctantly had nothing further to add and sat back down.

The judge then called both the accused to stand and told the haulage contractor, 'You have disgraced your family and brought total embarrassment to your entire family business!'

He then sentenced him to fifteen years' imprisonment, at which point the thirty-two-year-old haulage contractor burst into tears!

He then turned to the elderly accused, whose facial expression and his overall demeanour had changed dramatically, and said, 'You have already lost your own son to drug abuse and yet you continue to be involved in the possession and supplying of a class A drug, namely heroin. You may be a small cog in a big wheel, but you are every bit as much to blame. Therefore I'm sending out a message to others in the same position as you, who blatantly allow themselves to be involved in this way, that this court will not accept it. I therefore sentence you to eighteen years' imprisonment.'

The elderly man turned around to face his family, sitting in the court, and promptly fainted.

Mind you, so did half the Drug Squad sitting at the back of the court on hearing the sentences. This was a proper result!

Assisted by the escorting police officers in the dock, the elderly accused was helped to his feet just in time to hear the judge instruct the officers, 'Take them both down!'

Now call me old-fashioned, but that's what I call a sentence befitting the crime.

Well done, m'lord!

Isn't it a pity we don't have some consistency among our judges when sentencing persons convicted of or pleading guilty to serious crimes?

Maybe we should insist that our judges in Edinburgh and Glasgow swap courts to hear pleas every Friday after-noon!

The Jammy Dodgers

• • •

During the tour in Moscow with the folk band, we were contracted to perform nineteen concerts in twenty-one days.

Because of the schedule and the translation problems, I decided to take along our very own sound engineer, who would know our style of music and with whom we wouldn't have any communication problems.

I was able to secure the services of a very good and experienced engineer called Steve, who would work with us for a few months leading up to our departure and familiarise himself with our style.

The first week of our tour was going ahead as planned and, because of the publicity being created by our performances, we were receiving invitations to appear on Moscow TV chat shows, to perform and give interviews about our style of Scottish music and culture.

After one such appearance, we left the Moscow TV studio and were conveyed in our hired tour bus to a local hostelry for our lunch.

We arrived at the front door of the premises and were getting out the bus.

Two or three of us had alighted from the bus and the female translator accompanying us had got up from the front seat of the vehicle.

As she did so, Steve, who was a big lad of about twenty-three stone, was pulling himself up from his seat in the rear of the bus and holding on to the door lock.

Just at that moment, the female translator was passing

and, not seeing Steve still with his hand inside, grabbed hold of the sliding door and slammed it shut.

A loud scream bellowed out from Steve and, as I looked around, all I could see was our roadie wrenching the door open to reveal Steve's bloodied fingers.

'Quickly!' yelled the Russian tour manager. 'Bring him inside to we assess the damage to his hand!'

Poor Steve – his face had completely drained of colour with the severe pain he was obviously suffering.

As for our young female translator, she was totally distraught with what she had done, albeit completely by accident, but she was receiving more than her fair share of sympathy from the other band members – more so than Steve.

The roadie and the tour manager, tending to Steve, led him inside the venue.

Whilst being assisted, Steve gave the impression he was about to pass out with the excruciating pain.

As for me, I was trying to come to terms with the thought that Steve might not be able to continue with the tour, due to the severity of his injury, and how it would be near impossible to replace him.

Just at this point, Hamish, our fiddle and mandolin player, came up to me and said with genuine sincerity, 'Don't worry about it, boss, it could have been much, much worse.'

'How much worse could it get?' I asked him.

He paused for a moment before saying, 'Well! It could have been one of us!'

As he walked in the door ahead of me, I had to conceal my nervous laughter at his sick but very true observation.

Away, Ya Bum!

• • •

One afternoon a foreign, tanned man with film-star good looks, called at the police station to pay the money owed by him on a sheriff warrant which was being held in my divisional office.

He was accompanied by a very pretty young woman, at least ten years his junior, who was holding him tightly by the arm and, every now and again, kissing his cheeks and running her hands through his thick black shining hair.

'What's your name, sir?' I asked, though what I really wanted to say was, 'What's your name, ya dirty lucky, good-looking bastard?'

He replied with a straight face, 'Aenus!'

I thought I had misheard him, so I asked again, 'Can you just confirm your name for me, please? Did you say Anus?'

I mean to say, I've heard a few men refer to the love of their loins as an 'asshole', but who would christen their son 'Anus'?

But he replied, 'Correct. Aenus! Aenus Demitrius!'

Shit! He wasn't joking!

Isn't it amazing how some words and names translate completely different in our language?

A Busload of Trouble

. . .

Sometimes you have to relate the ugly side of policing and this is a prime example as a reminder that it's not always funny. It can be frightening and the humour conceals the serious side!

As a very young man with only three weeks' police service, I was instructed to attend the Thursday, Friday and Saturday of my first nightshift at Castlemilk police station.

Now, I lived in Renfrewshire and therefore had to leave my house at 7.15 p.m. in order to get a red Western bus to Clyde Street, then walk over the Suspension Bridge to Gorbals Cross to get a Glasgow Corporation bus to Castlemilk, to get there in time for my 9 p.m. start.

The first problem I encountered was on the Friday night, when I made my way to Renfrew Cross to await my bus in a crowded bus shelter. I was only there for a few minutes when a young man came running around the corner, closely followed by about five irate young men, screaming verbal abuse.

The man being pursued then had the misfortune to stumble and fall as he ran across the road, trying to avoid the traffic.

This allowed the nearest pursuer to catch up and aim a kick at him as he lay in the middle of the road.

Everyone in the bus shelter then looked at me to see what action I was going to take.

Now, I didn't start work until nine, but the members of the public around me didn't know that and because I was standing there in full uniform, they were all taking a back seat and I had to intervene and possibly take a beating from the pursuers because it was expected of me.

What to do? I ran at them and, pulling out my wooden baton, struck the first one on the upper arm and quickly lashed out with my boot, kicking another.

This caught the attackers completely by surprise and delighted my watching public, who shouted out their encouragement.

'C'mon, Constable, that's the way! Give them bloody laldy!'

Unbeknownst to my supporters, I wasn't just trying to protect the young victim – I was also trying to prevent myself from getting beaten up.

Standing over the victim, I lashed out again with my baton, striking out at anything that moved, and as I went to follow up with my brand new bulled black boots, the assailants, as one, turned and ran off.

I made a token attempt to chase them around the corner before stopping.

Returning to the scene, I was heaving a huge sigh of relief that it didn't turn out more serious when I walked around the corner in time to see two things.

Firstly, the young victim was up on to his feet and legging it down the main street and, secondly, the big red Western bus that I had been waiting on was being driven off from the bus stop, en route to Glasgow without me.

Left standing alone, it was as though nothing had ever happened.

Anyway, I sauntered slowly back over to the empty bus shelter to await another bus.

As I stood alone inside the shelter, shaking and with adrenalin still pumping through my veins, and trying to come to terms with what had taken place, I couldn't believe how quickly it had all ended.

Eventually, after about thirty minutes, another bus came along and although I was going to be late and unable to notify my shift sergeant, I was at least now on my way.

When I reached Clyde Street, I ran over the bridge to Gorbals Cross to catch the next bus, taking me to Castlemilk.

The nightmare I had encountered at Renfrew Cross was nothing compared to what I was about to endure, as along came the bus from hell.

Having just left Glasgow city centre, it was heaving with punters returning from a night of boozing in the pubs and clubs of the city centre.

I hadn't quite reached the bus stop but the driver, on seeing me, stopped to pick me up, and as I got on board I received a rude awakening as to why he wanted me on his bus.

It was sheer bedlam on board, with cursing, swearing, shouting and banging emanating from the top deck, and with about fifteen passengers standing downstairs, where there was standing room only for five. I soon realised that the downstairs overcrowding was the least of my worries.

'Thank goodness you're here, Constable. Just listen to that lot upstairs!' were the first words that greeted me from a nervous bus driver. 'They've been threatening passengers since we left the terminus. That's why they're all coming downstairs. I'm shitting mysel' wi' them on board!' he said, safe in his perplex vandal-proof cabin.

'How many of them are there?' I asked, sounding eager.

'Three that I know of, sir,' he replied. 'But one o' them is a big evil-looking bastard. I'm sorry for swearing, but I think you should go up and have a word with them and put them off the bus.'

'That's OK,' I said. 'Don't worry about it, I can see you're a bit nervous. Just let me go upstairs and check it out for myself.'

By this time I was beginning to feel slightly nervous, but I was angry as well and my adrenalin was beginning to flow again.

'OK, driver,' I said assuredly. 'I'm going to go upstairs first and warn them to stop the banging and shouting!'

'Good luck,' he said, before adding, 'Better you than me, son!' instilling total confidence in my next move.

I made my way upstairs, where I saw the three men responsible for the disturbance sitting drinking cans of beer at the back of the bus.

I decided to try the commonsense approach first.

'Right, guys, you've had a good night and I don't want to spoil it for you, but I need you to stop the noise, OK? You're disturbing the rest of the passengers. So, let us have no more shouting, swearing and banging, OK?'

They stared at me intently without uttering a word.

Hoping they were going to comply with my subtle approach, I made my way back downstairs, inwardly pleased with the response I felt I had achieved.

I had only just stepped down on to the platform when I heard one of them at the top of the stairs shout, 'Just keep fuckin' doing it and I'll chib the wee prick when he tries to come up the stairs!'

On hearing this threat, I turned to the driver and told him to put on his emergency alarm to try and attract the attention of any police patrols in the area.

'I'm sorry to tell ye this, Constable, but the emergency alarm doesn't work on this bus!' he informed me apologetically.

'Well, then!' I said. 'Let's head for the nearest police station and if you see any police cars on the way, signal them to stop!'

Moments later, the big evil-looking ned joined me on the downstairs platform. His head was shaven, which was totally unusual in the early seventies unless you'd been in Barlinnie Prison, and he had several scars, including a few large slashes on both cheeks.

Obviously a new tribe to Glasgow.

This guy's face had more lines on it than a Littlewoods football coupon!

However, my father used to always tell me, 'Son, never be afraid of anyone with a scarred face. Be more afraid of the person who gave him the scars!'

Now, at this point I was just praying these scars were not self-inflicted! Because this dude was scary, big-time!

Here I was, a young inexperienced police recruit, faced with a forty-year-old drunken hell raiser and I felt extremely threatened.

In fact, I was scared to the extent that the sweat was running down the inside of my trouser legs.

'Whit did you just tell that prick?' he demanded to

know, leaning his face into mine while breathing a foul combination of cigarettes and stale alcohol all over me.

I responded in the same aggressive manner. 'I told the prick to drive to the nearest police station.'

Now, that put the wind right up him . . . Not!

'Is that right?' he said, stepping even closer and putting his hand inside his breast coat pocket, revealing the tip of a wooden handle.

This made me so nervous it fired up my anger. I slipped my hand down the inside of my coat to grab my police baton, then my nerves got the better of me and I completely lost my composure and decided 'fight fire with fire', 'take the bull by the horns' or, better still, just 'flip yer lid!'

So I challenged him, 'Go for it, ya big arsehole! Bring out what ye're holding, but I'll tell you this, it better be a fuckin' sandwich, 'cause whatever ye produce, ye'll be fuckin' eating it!'

I'd now lost the plot, for this definitely was not Tulliallan Police College training methods; it was the art of discretion, fear and pure survival – speaking to him in the language he understood!

My backside was also operating on its own and was opening and closing like an elevator door at the entrance to a high-rise flat.

Meanwhile, out the corner of my eye, I caught a glimpse of the bus driver, who obviously thought I'd flipped my lid and was by now shitting himself along with most of the passengers, who had moved further inside the bus and turned their backs on me, to face the opposite way, lending their full support for the crazy young polis!

In other words: 'The young polis is a gemmy, but we don't really want tae be splashed with his blood when he's getting battered and chibbed by the big guy sporting a Barlinnie crop!'

As for the big guy, he was that thick he was still trying to digest what I had just said to him.

'Who the fuck dae you think ye're talking tae, ya wee prick?' he responded. Definitely annoyed – I could tell!

'You, ya arsehole!' I replied. Then I really lost the plot. 'In fact, let's just stop the bus right now and we'll get off for a proper square go. C'mon, just you and me, ya big diddy – let's see if you have any balls!'

I turned to the bus driver and said, 'Pull in and stop this fuckin' bus right now!'

The driver looked at me as if to say, 'Son, ye don't really want tae dae this,' but he reluctantly complied with my request (the obedient bastard!).

Once we had stopped, I opened the bus doors with the emergency lever.

'Right, let's go, ya big pussy!' I said to the ned, who willingly barged me right out of the way to get off the bus first, such was his eagerness to meet my challenge of a fight.

As he stepped off on to the pavement, I quickly closed the doors behind him and, holding them tightly closed, yelled to the driver, 'Quick, drive the bus! Go like fuck and don't stop for anything!'

As the bus pulled away from the stop, the ned realised I had conned him and started running after us, but the great Carl Lewis couldn't have caught this bus. Then I saw him running back to the bus stop and boarding another bus behind us.

Further along the road, having gained some distance, I told the driver to stop again and rushed upstairs for the other two neds, who were by now sitting like altar boys in a chapel choir, having lost their hardman mouthpiece.

'Right, you two, get yer arses off they seats. This is your stop!'

I grabbed them both and, pushing them down the stairs, ejected them from the bus, knowing full well they would also board the bus behind.

As the bus arrived at Castlemilk, I got off and ran like hell to the police station and, as luck would have it, the Land Rover crew were present and I related to them what had just taken place.

Mind you, I had to be told several times to calm down and slow down – being so nervous and shaken by the whole experience, I was talking in shorthand.

We all jumped into the Land Rover and drove to the Castlemilk terminus, where we arrived in time for the bus carrying the neds.

We apprehended the big evil-looking ned as he tried to leave the bus and found a butcher's cleaver concealed in his inside breast pocket.

This was the weapon that I was being threatened with on the bus.

It also transpired later, when checking him out, that he had recently been released on parole after having served a prison sentence for murder at HMP Barlinnie.

All this action whilst trying to get to my work and I hadn't officially started my police duty yet!

Needless to say, the hard man was found guilty and received another lengthy prison sentence, and in the next twenty-nine years of my police service, I never came across him again.

However, during the subsequent court case, the defence agent concentrated more on my aggressive action and threatening behaviour toward his client, placing him, as he put it, 'in a state of fear and alarm'.

As for the other two neds, well, they pleaded guilty to a charge of breach of the peace.

I still look back and believe I was very lucky that night to come out of two serious, separate situations totally unscathed, and it also taught me that when wearing your police uniform, you are on duty even when you're not, and you can never back down to anyone in a situation!

As an older colleague, Donald Hardie, once told me, 'Just remember, you are part of a much bigger gang and we must always win the fight!'

During the court case, I was mentioned by the sheriff in his summing up, for my 'excellent display of total profes-sionalism, in the face of what could only be described as extreme provocation'. If he only knew!

Incidentally, the bus driver, after much persuasion, and a woman passenger came forward and stood as witnesses to events on the bus that evening.

Two witnesses from a bus laden with fifty-plus passen-gers, and I know that obtaining witnesses to an incident taking place these days hasn't gotten any easier.

It is time we looked into the reason why the public are so reluctant to step forward and make themselves available to the police as witnesses.

I believe it is obvious – they are afraid, just like I was that night!

Good law-abiding citizens don't receive the protection expected from the police, the courts or the legal system in general.

Help Yourself

. . .

I stopped a driver for failing to comply with a red traffic light.

He immediately got out of his car and began swinging his arms about while ranting and raving at me, while telling me about the numerous procurator fiscal friends and solicitors he had and that he would be reporting me.

I remained very calm and, after he had stopped ranting, said, 'Right, now! If you're finished name-dropping, do you think you could tell me yours and let me see your driving licence?'

Off he went again, waving his arms about and shouting at the top of his voice, 'Just you wait! I'll have your job for this!'

'You wouldn't want my job, sir!' I replied calmly while writing his details into my notebook. 'The hours are long, the wages are crap and you have to deal with some right tosspots. Then again, I don't need to tell *you* that, sir – your friends in the procurator fiscal's office will no doubt have informed you first-hand!'

He Fancies You

• • •

Big Andy was the son of a former British army major and spoke like an officer himself, with clear diction and politeness.

When he appeared at the shift as a probationer, I was detailed to look after him.

One evening, having attended a disturbance at a local pub, Andy saw Rosie the barmaid, a cute, petite blonde girl with Meg Ryan looks and a bubbly personality to match.

He was immediately smitten by her.

'Go and chat to her and ask her out for a meal or a drink,' I said.

'I can't, Harry, I'm too shy,' he replied. 'Would you ask her for me? Please, Harry! Please.'

'OK,' I succumbed.

Like cupid, I sauntered over to Rosie and said, 'Rosie! My big mate over there is a bit embarrassed to ask you, because he's never been out with a woman before, apart from his mammy, but he'd really like to know if you would be interested in going out on a date with him.'

Rosie replied instantly, in her broad Glaswegian accent, 'I'd really love tae, pal, but right noo I'm sookin' the face aff a young guy fae the Calton!'

'Sookin' the face aff a guy'! Now that was a priceless response.

Ye just cannae beat that for an answer, can you?

The Cigar Man

• • •

Big Deke was a colleague of mine in the motorcycle section.

I say big, because he was six foot five and when he walked he was very conscious about it and tended to stoop.

He was a good guy, but he gave the impression of being quite a dour and unfriendly character.

Coupled with his deep-set eyes, he had an intimidating appearance; suffice to say you would rather he was on your side than against you.

It was a regular occurrence for all the police motor-cyclists to meet up at 3 p.m. every weekday in the canteen of the police training school in Oxford Street, prior to carrying out our parking ticket duties, or 'radial routes', as it was better known.

Due to big Deke's size and appearance, nobody ever played any practical jokes on him, but he would laugh wholeheartedly at everyone else when his partner 'Stook' played tricks on some of the others.

With this in mind, I decided to test big Deke for his sense of humour when he was the victim of the joke.

Deke wasn't a cigarette smoker, but was partial to the odd cigar.

Now, the exploding cigarettes were a regular thing with the rest of the guys, but an exploding cigar had never been done so, prior to going to the training school one day, I made a quick detour and stopped off at Tam Shepherd's joke shop in Queen Street in Glasgow city centre.

I told Tam what I was wanting and he supplied me with this genuine-looking top-of-the-range mega-cigar. This new type was just in and he hadn't even tried them out himself yet, but he guaranteed me it was a cracker, pardon the pun!

There was no way big Deke could resist it!

When I arrived at the canteen, most of the other bikers were seated around a table, sipping coffee and smoking cigarettes.

I pulled a chair over and sat directly opposite Deke. I then nonchalantly produced the cigar from my pocket and was slowly and deliberately unwrapping it as Deke looked on.

'That looks a beauty, wee man. Have you any more?' enquired Deke.

'Nope, sorry,' I replied. 'I only have the one and it's Cuban.' I then paused for a moment before continuing, 'But if somebody wants to give me a cigarette, you can have the cigar.'

Quick as a flash and totally unrehearsed, Deke's partner Stook took a cigarette packet from his jacket pocket and threw it over to me, saying, 'Here you go, Harry, have one of them and give Deke the cigar.'

'All right,' I said, handing the cigar to Deke, who accepted it gratefully.

I then sat back in my chair to watch his reaction to what was about to happen, as he confidently sniffed at it, then wrapped his big horrible lizard-like tongue around it to dampen it down, in order for it to burn slower.

His partner Stook put his lighter to the cigar as Deke sooked on the end of it several times before he satisfied himself it was properly lit.

He then relaxed back down, puffing away ecstatically.

'You can't beat a good cigar,' he said, viewing it in his hand. 'Rolled on the bare thighs of a beautiful half-naked Cuban woman – it ranks up there with an orgasm.'

Little did he know that this particular cigar was probably rolled on the bare arse of a Guy Fawkes look-a-like and he was about to experience an entirely different thrill!

After several puffs, Deke was really settling down to enjoying his big 'orgasmic' Cuban cigar and had just put it back up to his mouth, tempting his lips, when – BANG! – the end of the cigar blew up.

I couldn't contain myself as I burst out laughing, with several others around the table joining me in laughter at the look of surprise on his face, as his deep-set eyes almost popped out their sockets.

Fair dues to the big man, who did get a fright but accepted it in good humour as a practical joke.

'Were you part of this as well?' he asked Stook who had, after all, supplied me with the cigarette and Deke with a light.

'No!' he replied, rather unconvincingly. 'Definitely not!'

As the laughter died down and not about to ruin a good cigar, Stook cut off the end that was damaged and handed the cigar back to Deke. He then provided him with another light.

Before putting it to his mouth and puffing on it again, Deke enquired, 'Are you sure it's all right this time?'

Before I could respond, Stook spoke up, answering for me, 'Aye! They're just the same as the cigarette ones we bought – they only bang the once!'

Well, that's what *he* thought – and me, I might add.

Deke again sat back in his chair, puffing away as most of us around the table, particularly myself, watched with great interest.

'What are you all looking at?' he said. 'If you missed it the first time around then too bad. I don't do seconds!'

That's what he thought!

With perfect timing, he took a lingering puff on his cigar when . . . BANG!!

This time he got an even bigger fright, and this time he wasn't laughing. He pushed backwards on his chair, sliding along the tiled floor, and threw the cigar as far away as he could.

As it landed on the floor – BANG!!! – it went off again.

He then turned to Stook and said, 'Ya sleekit big bastard, you're out of order doin' that!'

Stook shook his head and tried to insist that he had nothing to do with it, but Deke was convinced Stook had been involved in specially arranging it.

'You provided Harry with a cigarette and provided me with a light twice – you set me up and I know it! You were too quick to give him a fag!' he said.

No matter how much Stook tried, he couldn't convince Deke that he had no involvement, and I certainly wasn't going to help him get out of it.

As I quietly slipped out of the canteen, Stook was still pleading his innocence but to no avail!

Not only did I get big Deke, but I also managed, through his eagerness to help out, to deflect the blame on to his partner Stook!

Good one, Harry boy!

It's a Knockout

...

One night my regular neighbour on the Shawlands Cross beat was off on long-term sick leave so they organised a senior cop from the Gorbals to partner me.

Now this cop was a good guy called Roy Dunsmore, who had great experience and just happened to be a former boxer.

Roy had a good sense of humour and a likeable way of dealing with members of the public who had drunk more than they could hold and were becoming a nuisance to everyone.

Such was the case on this particular night, when we encountered two spoiled brats who were set on trying to enter a local nightclub.

The bouncers refused them entry.

As this was obviously something they were not accustomed too, they were name-calling the stewards and becoming totally argumentative towards them.

On seeing what was developing, Roy and I went over and intervened.

Roy put his arm around one of their waists and pulled him gently aside.

'C'mon now, boys, I think you've had a good night and drank your last pub dry. So, how about heading home to your bed and sleeping it off?'

The one that Roy was holding on to began to struggle free and said, 'Who the hell do you think you are talking too? I don't drink, so you can apologise to me right now!'

Slightly bemused by this statement, Roy replied, 'Well,

you both do a good impersonation of a pair of muppets or somebody who *does* drink!'

'Are you deaf?' said the other brat, butting in. 'He said he doesn't drink,' and, leaning over to look at Roy's shoulder insignia number, he added sarcastically, 'Cunt-stable!'

Then they both began giggling like a pair of nursery schoolchildren.

Roy's attitude changed right there and then.

'OK, boys, you've had your fun. Now I'm telling you both to move along.'

They looked at Roy intently for a moment before bursting out laughing again.

This was not a very good idea! Not in front of Roy, that's for sure!

'I think you pair of mummy's boys better head for home and not say any more!' Roy warned them.

The first one replied rather indignantly, 'Who are you calling mummy's boys? I'll get you the sack, you pleb! Do you know who my father is?'

Roy promptly responded, 'So that's it, ya wee spoilt bastard? *You* don't even know who yer faither is? Well, I'm no' surprised – I wouldn't own up to it either!'

At that, Roy grabbed both their arms and led them away before releasing them, to walk unassisted.

'Final warning to you boys, go home now!' he said in a firm voice.

'Who do you think you are, you pig? My family could buy and sell you!' said the first one, as he lunged at Roy, grabbing hold of his arm and pulling at him.

Roy shrugged him off, but he was persistent and lunged at Roy again.

Big mistake!

As nice as you like and as quick as a flash, Roy pulled him around and hit him with a short, sharp, right hook to the jaw.

The spoilt little brat collapsed like a deck of playing cards.

His legs were like rubber and I had to assist Roy in holding him up.

He was slavering at the mouth as he tried to talk but was making absolutely no sense.

The other brat quickly sobered up on seeing his friend collapse.

'What happened to him?' he enquired, unaware of what had occurred.

'I think your pal is a wee secret drinker, son!' said Roy as he sat the boy down, propping him up against a lamp post. 'I think it's gone straight to his head!'

'What will I do?' he asked pathetically.

To which Roy replied with great satisfaction, 'Well, if I was you I'd get a taxi and take him home to mum and dad, before the same thing hits you as well!'

Roy then looked at me, winked and said, 'Know what I mean, 'Arry?'

What a Penis!

· · ·

I must tell you a story my mother told me after she had returned from her 'Athritic Club', where musical entertainment had been provided by some local female church choir singers and a male musician.

My mother is eighty years young and still relatively active, but sometimes gets her words wrong.

Such was the case when she was describing the entertainment, and she was totally enthusiastic about their performance.

'They were absolutely marvellous singers and what a penis they had with them. I've never seen a penis like this – it was fantastic and a born entertainer. He could perform anywhere. And he did them all – Winifred Atwell, Mrs Mills, Bobby Crush and even Nina Simone!'

I later had to explain to her that he was in fact a 'pianist' and she then explained that the three ladies and man referred to were also well-known pianists and not fellow members of her 'Athritic Club'!

Mind you, she also said the fire alarm was activated during the show and they all had to 'ejaculate' the building!

Lost Luggage
• • •

I attended a call at the house of an elderly man who had returned home from a holiday in Ireland and had uplifted the wrong suitcase from the baggage collection hall at the airport.

On my arrival at the address given, the man, who spoke with an Irish accent, greeted me at the door and invited me in.

'That's the suitcase there!' he said, pointing to a bright green case lying in the middle of the lounge floor.

It was a very unusual colour for a suitcase and I would have thought it would have been very difficult to make a mistake.

'Have you tried to open it?' I asked him.

'No, sir, to be honest, that I haven't. As soon as I noticed it wasn't mine, I called the police,' he replied. 'And sure enough, you arrived! I haven't tried opening it, that's for sure, but I think it's locked anyway,' he replied.

'Are you positive it isn't your suitcase, sir?' I asked. 'Are you sure you don't recognise any of these stickers on the front? Butlins? Pontins? Rothesay? Dunoon?'

'No, sir, to be honest with you again, I don't. Although I do have some stickers on my case, but I don't recognise any of these ones. Definitely not!' he replied in a positive manner.

I asked if I could see his suitcase key and I tried it in the lock of the 'wrong' suitcase he had collected.

Surprise, surprise, the case opened easily at the turn of the key.

As I opened it out to check its contents, the elderly man leaned over my shoulder to look inside.

'B'Jesus, would you look at that! My suitcase key fits it, that's amazing! You would think they would issue different keys for different cases,' he said. 'Amazing!'

I began removing some of the articles of clothing from the case.

'Let me know if you recognise anything, Mr Barrett,' I said, holding up some of the shirts.

'I will that, sir, but if it's not my case, I won't be recognising any of it!' he replied assuredly.

I continued to remove some more articles of clothing from the case, searching for something that would assist me in identifying the rightful owner.

'Good God, would you look at that shirt!' he said.

'Is it yours?' I asked. 'Do you recognise it?' I held it up for him to see.

'Jesus, no, sir! To be honest, I'm thinking who could wear such a ridiculous-looking shirt? That's frightening!' he replied. 'This person should be locked up, if you ask me!'

I knelt back down and continued removing articles of clothing, shaving kit and toiletries. Then I came across an envelope containing family photographs.

As I removed them I handed them over to Mr Barrett.

'What about these photos? Do you recognise any of the people in them?'

Again, he replied in his soft Irish brogue, 'No, sir, to be honest, I don't know them at all. I mean, how would I know them when it's not my suitcase?'

At that point he gave me the photographs back and, as I flipped through them, I saw a picture of an elderly man holding a young child in his arms.

'Mr Barrett, is that not you in the picture holding up a small boy?' I asked, handing over the photograph.

'No, sir, not at all. To be honest, it looks a bit like me, but the man in the photograph looks much older and I certainly don't have any children!' he said, totally convincingly.

A further search of the case revealed name and address labels in the name of James Barrett.

'Well, who is James Barrett then, Mr Barrett? Is it not a coincidence that this case should belong to a Mr Barrett also? Are you sure it isn't yours?'

I looked at him for a moment, waiting for an answer.

'No, sir, definitely not. My name is Patrick Barrett, I'm positive about that!' he replied. 'Obviously this fellow is going to have the same name as me, because he has the same suitcase as well, but I certainly don't know of him!'

Convinced there was something not right with Mr Barrett and that this was indeed his suitcase, I asked him to produce some form of identification with regards to himself.

'To be sure, I can't do that, sir!' he replied immediately.

'Why not, Mr Barrett? This is your house,' I said. 'Or have you entered into the wrong house as well?'

He replied back, totally convincingly, 'Exactly, sir, and that's why I called you. When I lost my suitcase with all my luggage, I also lost my entire identification and now

I'm left with a suitcase belonging to someone else with the same name as me and keys to their house!'

Suddenly, I heard the front door opening and in walked a woman in her early forties. As I watched her enter, she looked at me with complete surprise, then towards Mr Barrett.

'What's wrong? What's up?' she enquired in a panic. Then, turning to Mr Barrett, she asked, 'Oh, Dad, what have you been doing this time?' before turning back around to face me. 'What's happened, officer? What has he done now?'

After a well-deserved cup of tea for me, 'the demented polis', I informed her why I was there.

The woman explained that she was Mr Barrett's daughter and he had been away for a week staying with her sister, who lived in Ireland.

Mr Barrett had been diagnosed the previous year with signs of Alzheimer's disease and his condition was notably deteriorating rapidly.

The amazing thing was, he was a Glaswegian through and through and had only developed his Irish accent, which he had brilliantly perfected, during his week's holiday at his other daughter's home in Ireland.

Also, as it turned out, his name was indeed James Barrett and Patrick just happened to be the name of his grandson, who was the small boy in the photograph with him.

Someone to Talk to

...

Having broken down outside a house, a woman came out to see if she could help me. I informed her it was OK as I had a mobile telephone and had already called for a recovery vehicle.

The woman then offered me tea or coffee, the use of her toilet and generally remained outside in her garden, leaning on her garden gate, talking with me until the recovery vehicle arrived.

As I was leaving, I thanked her for her help and she replied, 'Don't mention it, son. It's only when some poor bugger like yersel' breaks down that I get a chance tae talk to somebody!'

Different Strokes

...

Two detective officers were playing a round of golf when one asked, 'How has your week been?'

The other one was lining up to tee off. 'I've been kept busy with a murder inquiry!' he replied.

'A murder? What happened?' said the first one.

'Some young up-and-coming professional golfer beat his girlfriend to death with a golf club!' he responded.

'That's dreadful!' said the other, who then paused for moment before asking, 'How many strokes did he take?!'

The Frying Pan Man

· · ·

'Biffo' McMahon worked out of a small station in Cambuslang. He was aptly named because he looked like Biffo the cartoon bear!

Like most of the cops working out of the station, Biffo liked to cook his own meals in the office and was a great man for his bacon and eggs.

One of the cops on my shift had donated a frying pan and some cooking pots for the use of the office staff.

However, on several occasions when we wanted to use it, we often discovered it had been put away in the cupboard without being cleaned after use. So eventually I complained and asked who it was that used the frying pan, returning it unwashed?

Every person on every shift said the same thing: 'It wisnae me! It wisnae me!'

Mr Bloody Nobody did it again!

Eventually I got fed up when I went to use it one day and it resembled a dry lavvy, or should I say lavatory. It was totally boggin'.

There were even wee feet marks where the mice had been practising their Torvill and Dean bolero act and skating about in the grease!

Mind you, the entire office was that old and dirty, even the mice ran about wi' dungarees on!

Anyway, I picked the frying pan up and put it in the bin.

Lo and behold, the very next day, I opened up the kitchen cupboard and there, taking pride of place, was the binned frying pan.

Bugger that, I thought as I picked it up, and this time I threw it into a refuse bin outside the police station's back door.

After my shift was finished, I enjoyed the next two days off before returning to take up nightshift duty.

I logged myself on duty and read over my duty officer journal to see what had been happening during my days off.

Then I went through to the kitchen area to make a cup of coffee. As I opened the cupboard, I couldn't believe my eyes, as there, once again, was the condemned frying pan.

It was the Scottish equivalent of an Australian boomerang – it just kept coming back. A bit like the shift sergeant's wife – every night he threw her out along wi' the cat, but she would return home the very next morning.

However, that's another story.

Anyway, back to the frying pan!

I took it out, opened the back door of the station and threw it along the yard, behind some lock-ups. They'll never find it there, I thought to myself.

How wrong was I?

The following evening I entered the office and there on the kitchen stove was the offending frying pan with nine lives!

On hearing me enter the rear of the office, Biffo came running through and, seeing me, said, 'Don't you dare throw that frying pan out again and don't dare deny it – I know it was you!'

'Frying pan!' I said. 'That manky, all-stick metal pan should carry a health warning! My cat's box is cleaner!'

'No, it is not!' said Biffo, trying to sound like a voice of authority. 'Noo I've told my gaffer about it and if you throw that frying pan oot again, he's putting you on paper and reporting you for damaging police property.'

'Is that right? Well, you tell him to go ahead, ya nutcase, but if ye leave it out again, it's for the off. It's minging and it's stinking out the bloomin' office! Anyhow, it was my shift that supplied it, no' the polis!'

A few days later, poor old Biffo was off duty when his shift members left out the offending frying pan. I couldn't resist it, so I gave it a new place to reside – in the refuse dump at Cathkin Braes, in the back of beyond!

Poor old Biffo. Apparently he was like a bear with a sore head on his return to duty, but he never made any mention of it again.

I would also like to think that I made several of the resident office mice homeless!

That Crap

• • •

Which reminds me of a joke my son Scott told me about two dung beetles that climbed on to a steaming hot pile of fresh cow manure.

One lifted his legs and farted.

The other one said in disgust, 'Aw, for goodness' sake, Jimmy, can ye no' see I'm trying to eat here!'

Sign Language for the Stupid

• • •

One day I was patrolling the East End of Glasgow on my police motorcycle and decided to have a little jaunt through the famous Glesca Barras, to check things out and show a police presence.

I was riding through on my own when this stockily built drunk man came out from the doorway of a leather clothes shop and jumped in front of me.

As I stopped my bike, he stood in front of me and began to make grunting and growling noises at me.

He then stepped closer and, before I could react, he grabbed hold of the front of my full-facial motorcycle helmet. As he did, he began to pull my head from side to side, yelling and screaming in my face.

While doing this, he caused me to twist and strain my neck.

All the time he was doing it, I was unable to defend myself properly, having to hold on to my motorcycle to avoid falling over. I was also extremely embarrassed, with so many shoppers looking on.

Finally I managed to draw his attention with my eyes and he stopped pulling at my helmet and screaming in my face.

As he looked at me intently, I pulled my helmet down in order to reveal my mouth to him.

I then asked him, very clearly and deliberately, 'CAN YOU READ LIPS?'

He nodded 'yes' and made a growling, screaming noise to accompany it.

'GOOD!' I replied. 'NOW READ THIS VERY CARE-FULLY!' I then mouthed to him in silence, so that no one else could hear, 'GET TO FUCK OUT MY SIGHT, BEFORE I GET OFF THIS BIKE AND KICK YOU UP AND DOWN THE STREET, YA DUMB BASTARD!'

He stared at me, eyeball to eyeball, and I was preparing myself for him to make another physical attack, when the owner from the leather clothes shop came out, took him by the arm and, using sign language, told him it would not be advisable to hang about.

Having changed his mind, the snarling male was then ushered away by the man from the leather shop, thus preventing any further confrontation!

As it was, he turned out to be a real pain in the neck for me!

A New Type of Mixer

• • •

My colleague O'Reilly and his wife called at my house one evening for a social night.

As they sat down in the lounge, I asked O'Reilly's wife, Mary, if she would like a drink.

'I'll have a vodka, please, Harry,' she responded.

'Certainly! What would you like with your vodka?' I asked.

'Anything at all!' she replied.

Which prompted me to say, 'OK, Mary! How about a shag, then?'

Strictly Private and Confidential
· · ·

I worked with a sergeant who was nicknamed 'Harpic' for the obvious reason – he was completely 'right around the bend'.

One day he was doing the appraisal of a cop on my shift – this was commonly known as your yearly MOT.

The sergeant was desperate to have this officer continue in his present role as a tutor cop, partnering a new recruit to the force and teaching him the ropes, using all his experience.

As it was, this cop had spent the last three years performing this duty – what we called 'nappy changing' – and was seeking a new challenge for himself.

During his appraisal with Harpic, he emphasised his reluctance to continue in this role and expressed a desire to move on and try something different.

The sergeant appreciated his views and reluctantly agreed, accepting his request for a change.

Later the same day, the cop had occasion to enter the sergeant's room to collect some urgent despatches for police headquarters, and while in there going through them he noticed a file with his name on it, marked '<u>Strictly Private and Confidential</u>'.

Curious to know what the file contained about him, he opened it up and discovered that Harpic had blatantly ignored his previous request for a change and recommended that he continue in his present role as a tutor cop.

The irate cop returned to see Harpic, and displayed his annoyance at him for ignoring his earlier request for a change.

Harpic, however, was more concerned about the fact that the cop had opened and read over a report that was clearly marked '**<u>Strictly Private and Confidential</u>**' and strenuously made the cop aware that 'strictly private and confidential' meant exactly what it said and he'd had absolutely no right to open it!

After a heated argument regarding what had been discussed and what had been written, the cop returned to my office totally fuming and related the entire incident with regards to the 'strictly private and confidential' file about him and its contents!

Several days later, I was sending out reminders to the members on my shift who owed money and were in arrears with their subscription to the pools coupon syndicate that I was responsible for organising and paying.

I decided, as a total wind-up for Harpic, to obtain 'private and confidential' envelopes and send out the reminders with a letter stating, 'Don't let Harpic see this note, but give him the impression that it is an important despatch that you have received and it is solely for your eyes only! TELL HIM NOTHING!'

All the brown envelopes were clearly marked '**<u>Strictly Private and Confidential</u>**' when they landed on Harpic's desk the following day, to be distributed by him among the members of his shift.

I was told that his facial expression was priceless, when he started to read the labels and hand out the despatches at the muster of the shift.

For the rest of the night he hung around like a bad smell, trying to find out the contents of the envelopes.

However, he was informed by each and every one of his shift that the letters were 'strictly private and confidential', and he of all people should know the significance of that!

He was completely demented for days about it and, dare I say . . . I managed to drive Harpic clean round the bend!

The Cycle Period

Arthur was a young police officer on my shift who had a fancy for the civilian female station assistant, but he was always slightly shy to talk to her.

One day, he plucked up the courage to ask her out.

'Hi, Jean!' (She used to be a cleaner!) 'Would you like to come back to my apartment after your shift finishes for a drink?'

Jean replied, 'I would love to, but I've got my menstrual cycle.'

'That's OK!' replied Arthur. 'We can park it at the back of the police station and you can collect it later!'

By the way, he recently announced to the shift that he was bisexual.

So, he now doesn't know whether he's Arthur or Martha, and to add insult to injury, he now gets a knock-back from both sexes.

Got a Light, Mate?

• • •

Stuart Bailey was a cop from Lanarkshire who liked a dram and a cigarette.

One evening he was standing in his local pub, prior to the new smoking ban, having a quiet drink, and had just lit up a cigarette when a stranger standing at the bar next to him, holding a cigarette in his hand, asked Stuart, 'Excuse me, mate, do you have a light there, please?'

Stuart looked him straight in the eye and replied, 'Yes, I do thanks!' then turned his back to him.

The stranger tapped Stuart on the shoulder and asked, 'Well, do you think you could give me a light, please?'

Stuart turned around to face the stranger and said, 'Naw! I'm not giving you a light! Now bugger off!'

The stranger remarked, 'There's no need to be so rude! After all, I was only asking you for a light for my cigarette!'

Stuart responded, 'Is that right, mate? Whit's your name?'

The stranger answered, 'It's Richard, but my friends call me Dick for short!'

'Well, Dick, just let me analyse your request for a moment. Now, you're asking me to give you a light for your cigarette, is that correct?'

'That's correct,' confirmed Dick.

Stuart continued with his analysis, 'Right, then! So, I give you a light and you offer me a cigarette as a polite gesture and I take the cigarette off you. Next thing is, we start talking. Y'know, the usual pish! "Where are you from?" I'll ask, and you'll reply, "Oh, I'm from such and such a place, but I'm just up here on business," and we'll get right involved in conversation.

'Then I'll go to buy a drink and I'll feel obliged to ask you if you want one and you'll say, "Yes, please, Stuart. I'll have a whisky and a half-pint of lager." And while I'm getting them in, you'll give me a fag and I'll give you another light.

'Then it'll be your turn to order up the drinks and so on and so forth and we'll both end up totally pished. So I'll ask you how you got over here. And you'll reply, "Oh, I drove over in the car. I'm staying in a hotel in Glasgow."

'Then I'll feel terrible for getting you so drunk and I'll say, "Well, you cannae drive yer car like that, Dick," and I'll invite you back to my house, which is in walking distance o' the pub, for a cup o' coffee and when we get back there, my missus will take one look at your face and say to me, "Stuart! You cannae let that Dick drive a car in that condition. We better let him stay the night and sleep it off." So I'll invite you to stay the night and sleep it off.

'But there's a slight problem with that synopsis, Dickie boy. You see, my house only has two bedrooms – the missus and me sleep in one and my innocent, gorgeous, voluptuous, seventeen-year-old daughter Britney sleeps in the other one.

'So you, Dickie my boy, would have to get yer head down for the night on the sofa in the lounge, with the spare duvet o'er ye. And sure as shite in a wean's minging nappie, during the night, ya randy bastard, yer old hormones will start twitching and ye'll get up and go for a wander.

'With yer aroused boaby sticking oot in front o' ye like a

divining rod leading the way, you'll go sneaking upstairs into my innocent, gorgeous, voluptuous, seventeen-years-old daughter Britney's bedroom for a gander at her pure, lily-white, untouched body, and while she's lying there like an angel, in a deep sleep, ye'll slip into bed beside her and have yer evil end away!

'My innocent young daughter will be totally oblivious to this and just think she's been having her first sexually explicit erotic dream during the night, having never met you.

'Next morning, the wife and I will get up out of bed and discover that you, Dickie my boy, have buggered off in a fast black afore we're even down the stairs.

'Oh, aye, and another thing – my wife will be so worried about you, she'll say, "I wonder what time that Dick got up this morning," and, "I hope that Dick had some breakfast afore he left the house," and, best of all, "Dick must have been 'aroused' early – I just hope he wasn't frozen stiff with the cold during the night." Frozen? Maybe. Stiff? Definitely!

'Nothing else will be said and I'll think everything in the garden is rosy. Totally unaware, of course, that during the night you have planted yer family seedlings, ya manky bastard!

'My young, innocent, gorgeous, voluptuous daughter Britney will suddenly, and without trying too hard, gain more weight than Bridget Jones! And instead o' getting ready for the school prom dance, she'll look like she's getting ready to go sumo wrestling with the Wang Hung Lo brothers!

'Then nine months down the line, guess what? We're Granny and Grandpa Bailey, to a wee Dick, who my once innocent, gorgeous and voluptuous daughter Britney has just dropped off at the Royal Maternity Hospital, compliments of a Mr Richard (call me Dick) Boner, who just happens to have done a Lord Lucan!'

At this point, an agitated Dick interrupted Stuart, 'I won't do that! I won't! I won't! I promise you I won't!'

To which Stuart replied, 'Ye're fuckin' right ye won't! 'Cause yer no' getting a bastardin' light! *Now, fuck off, ya pervert!*'

Answers from Real Police Scotland Exams

• • •

'Prevarication on oath – lying under oath in the belief that not believing or recognising God allows the witness/accused a get-out clause'!

I don't think so!

Boxer Shorts

• • •

I answered the telephone in the office and was greeted with the following, 'Harry! It's wee Dougie. I've got a bit of information for you about that big cop Davie on your shift!'

'What information are you talking about, Dougie?' I enquired.

'Information that he's shagging an auld bird from Dalmarnock!' replied Dougie.

'You're way off the track there, Dougie, 'cause Davie wouldn't know where Dalmarnock is, never mind an old woman!' I said. 'He's from the country and he hardly knows Glesca!'

'I'm telling you, it's him,' he reiterated.

'No way!' I said. 'Anyway, who told you this?'

'My daughter Karen!' he replied. 'She recognised him when she was going up her pal's tenement close. She saw him from the stair-landing window and could see right into the house. She even saw him taking aff his kit. She described him to a T!'

'How did she know he was a polis?' I asked him.

'Because he still had his uniform on,' he replied. 'She watched him taking aff his kit and folding it neatly before hanging it up on the door!'

'Is she sure it was him?' I asked again.

'Definitely!' he confirmed confidently. 'She even saw his big baggy boxer shorts, they were a dead giveaway!'

'Well, I don't believe it!' I said, before putting the phone down.

A few days passed and in that time I had been out twice for a drink with big Davie and he had never mentioned it.

However, wee Dougie called at the police station to do a minor repair on my car.

Whilst he was there, I invited him into the back of the office for a cup of tea.

We sat for a short time talking and he was asking me if big Davie had made any mention about what he had said about him when the door of the office opened and in walked big Davie himself.

After a bit of idle chat, Dougie couldn't contain himself and said to Davie, 'Are you shagging an auld bird from Dalmarnock?'

Davie replied, 'Me? I don't know the Dalmarnock area and I certainly don't know any old birds from there either!'

Dougie then changed his tactics. 'Well, I'll bet you a tenner you're wearing boxer shorts.'

Davie looked at him with a puzzled expression on his face and said, 'What?'

Dougie produced a £10 note from his pocket.

'A tenner. I'm betting you a tenner you're wearing boxer shorts!'

Davie shook his head and refused to accept his bet. This made Dougie all the more determined.

'Right, then,' he said, producing another £10 note from his pocket. 'I'll make it twenty pounds you're wearing big saggy, baggy white boxer shorts!'

'I'm not betting you, Dougie!' Davie responded. 'You're mad!'

At that, Dougie looked over at me and winked. 'See, I told you! He knows I'm right!' said an ecstatic Dougie. Then, holding his hands up, he stated, 'I rest my case!'

'I know you're right about what?' enquired big Davie.

'I'm right when I say you're wearing baggy boxers! You were observed, as we say!' replied a rather cocky Dougie.

At that, big Davie said, 'How much are you betting me?'

Dougie responded immediately, 'I'm betting you twenty quid!'

'Why not make it fifty?' said Davie. 'If you're that confident!'

Dougie paused for a moment before responding in a confident and cocky manner, 'Fifty quid it is!'

The words were hardly out of Dougie's mouth before big Davie walked over and locked the back door to the office.

'Just in case it's a set-up and yer pal in the motor thinks he can barge in here and take a picture o' me with my trousers down at my ankles!' he said to Dougie.

He then unbuckled his belt and slowly dropped his trousers to his knees, revealing a neat pair of tight-fitting Y-fronts.

He then looked at Dougie and said, 'I think you, Mr Big Mouth, owe me an apology!' He paused before holding out his hand. 'Oh, and I'll just have my fifty quid, thank you very much.'

As he took the money, big Davie said in utter disgust, 'Now, I suggest you fuck off out of this police station before I place another bet with you that you spend the rest of the day here . . . in a polis cell!'

Soup on the Menu

• • •

I received a call one day to attend a road accident, whereby a vehicle had struck a male pedestrian.

On my arrival at the location, I saw the emergency ambulance leaving with its blue lights flashing and its siren blaring, en route to the accident and emergency department at Glasgow Royal Infirmary.

While speaking to witnesses at the accident spot, I learned that the injured man had been drinking in a local pub only minutes earlier and had left to make his way home.

Once outside, he'd noticed a large van being driven down the road towards him and had informed his friend, who was accompanying him, that he knew the van driver.

'Let's give him a fright!' he said.

At that, he bent down and made his way out between two parked cars, totally out of view of the oncoming driver.

As the vehicle neared his position, he leapt out in front of it. The oncoming driver swerved at the last minute to avoid him, but unfortunately he struck the pedestrian on the head with the large wing mirror. *Scud*!

The pedestrian immediately dropped on to the road like a sack of potatoes, bleeding profusely from a serious head wound.

The friend, who was relating the story to me, then said, 'You must know him!' and told me his name and address.

As it was, I was not familiar with the name of the injured pedestrian so I contacted the office regarding his identity.

The duty sergeant, Jim Charlton, contacted me right back. 'Ya beauty!' he said, adding, 'I just hope its nothing trivial!'

He told me our injured pedestrian was in fact a rat from his former beat area, who loaned money to struggling families and charged them excessively high interest rates.

He was also known to threaten the families for late or non-payment, and was not averse to using excessive physical and torturous violence toward them to make a point.

In other words, he was what is commonly known as a loan shark!

The sergeant said that none of the families he tortured and whom he charged extortionate interest were willing to come forward and report matters to the police for fear of more serious repercussions.

With this in mind, I attended at the Royal Infirmary, where I was informed that, due to the serious head injury he had sustained, he'd been transferred to the neurosurgical unit.

I returned to the police station to submit my report of the entire incident.

A few days later, I followed up on the progress of the injured pedestrian by calling personally at the hospital to check on him.

At the nurses' station, I was informed that his head injuries were serious and, if he survived them, he would require twenty-hour-care because of the brain damage he had sustained.

I was then shown into the ward, where I saw him with what appeared like a budgie's cage fitted over his head, with metal spikes affixed and protruding from his shaven skull.

When I returned to the station, Sergeant Charlton met with me in the corridor.

'Oh, by the way, Harry! How's that wee rat who scudded the van with his head and damaged the driver's wing mirror?' he asked sarcastically.

'It's not looking too good for him! In fact, if I was to ask you to sum up the one word that covers cabbage, turnip, carrot and Brussels sprouts, what would it be?' I asked him.

As he paused for a moment, a young probationary constable shouted over in complete innocence, 'Gravy!'

As we both looked around at him in disbelief, the sergeant said in a dismissive but smug voice, 'Vegetable!' He continued, 'Well, that will come as a great relief to a lot of families in Bridgeton, and I can't say I'm sorry to hear it. He was an evil little bastard who made a lot of families suffer!'

'Was he that bad?' I asked.

'Definitely that bad!' he replied. 'However, I suppose his "Rat Pack" family will still benefit from him!'

I looked at the sergeant, seeking an explanation!

He then leaned forward, looked me straight in the eye and said, 'They'll never be short of a vegetable when they come to make a pot of soup!' He then walked off singing to himself, 'Boiled beef and carrots, boiled beef and carrots! Onion bonnie banks and onion bonnie braes . . .'

He stopped, looked back at me and said, 'Hey! What about, as a starter, soup de jour? Loan shark soup!'

Daddy's Car
• • •

One night, on a backshift with my partner Joe Doran, we were working an area from the infamous Gorbals up to Eglinton Toll.

While walking the beat, Joe informed me he had attended a call the previous day and had met with a good-looking woman whom he had arranged to meet later that evening, during our shift.

After we had been in for our refreshment period and were returning to our beat, we were walking along the road when a rather nifty little sports car pulled up beside us. It was Joe's date!

'Hop in,' she said. 'My dad gave me his new sports car.'

Joe looked at me and said, 'I'll see you later, Harry! Give me a shout if you need me or if the gaffer's looking for me.'

As he squeezed himself into the neat little car, he said, 'I'll be up at Bert's place!'

This was an area of his beat near Eglinton Toll.

'Either way, I'll meet you at about nine thirty, outside the bingo!' he added.

Off they went, while I continued with my solo patrol.

After about an hour and a half of walking about myself, I met with the crew from the divisional Land Rover and was chatting away with them, not mentioning anything about Joe, when they received a call to return to the police station and uplift the shift inspector and sergeant.

This was the evening ritual as the supervisors were driven around the beat areas, whereby they would sign the officers' notebooks to the effect that they were present on their beat patrolling at a specific time.

Knowing this, I made my way to the bingo to meet up with Joe. After ten or fifteen minutes, there was no sign of Joe and I could hear over my personal radio the gaffers calling up the locations of other cops near by.

I quickly made my way up to the area where I knew Joe would be and, sure enough, she was parked up in a lane.

The windows were all steamed up, so I knocked on the roof of the car and said, 'Joe! Joe! Time to go, the gaffers are out signing notebooks!'

Joe's hand rubbed away at the steamy driver's window to expose what appeared like some erotic action had taken place.

Just as he did so, I received a call from the controller seeking our location.

I said to Joe that I would walk down and meet them, giving him the time required to compose himself.

As I was walking away, I heard the car engine start up and, as I looked back, I saw it being reversed at speed out of the lane then – CRASH! BANG! WALLOP! – the windows were so steamed up that the driver couldn't see properly out the back window and she collided with a lamp post, crumpling the boot lid and rear bumper.

As they both got out the car to investigate the damage, I did a B52 and buggered off sharpish!

I arrived at the location seconds before the gaffers, and while I was having my notebook signed they asked me where Joe was.

I was about to make up some excuse to cover for Joe when the radio controller called the inspector.

'Just to inform you that 365' (Joe's divisional number) 'has come across a road accident and is in the process of dealing with it,' the controller informed him.

'Are there any injuries?' enquired the inspector.

Which I spontaneously answered, 'No!'

As the inspector turned to look at me, the controller confirmed there were no injuries.

'Roger,' replied the inspector. 'Tell him we'll see him back at the office with his report.'

He then looked at me and asked, 'How did you know that?'

'I'm psychic!' I replied, smiling confidently.

As they drove off, I quickly made my way back to Joe and on my arrival I had to restrain myself from laughing out loud when I saw the damage sustained to Daddy's new sports car, bent around the lamp post as if part of it.

Joe was doing his best to console his girl as she wept uncontrollably. He even came up with an excuse for her to tell Daddy.

While Joe was comforting her, his new burd had gone from erotic to erratic and was struggling free every now and again to slap him about the head and body.

At this point I decided it was time to leave the two love-birds to sort it out in their own way, while I went and had a cup of coffee at the local bingo hall.

So, psychic or not, I was wrong! There *were* injuries sustained . . . but it was Joe that sustained them, as his inconsolable burd physically assaulted him!

As a finale to the story, Joe promised to attend a driving school for lessons, to improve HIS dreadful reversing skills, no doubt!!

Driving with My Eyes Shut

• • •

Back in 1975, I was attending Tulliallan Police College for a three-week advanced driving course.

My instructor was a sergeant from Aberdeen called Doug Keil, with whom I formed a good relationship.

Having completed various parts of the course – driving in open country roads, town roads, motorways, skidpan, manoeuvring, mechanics and the three written exams – it was the final week of driving before our final three test drives.

Doug was trying to get one of the students in my car to relax a bit more and smooth out his driving skills.

As a compliment of how well I was driving during the three-week course, Doug decided I should drive, to demonstrate to Philip how it should be done.

I took over the driving and was very quickly into my stride, commentating on all around me and in front as I careered along the road at excessively high speeds.

Eventually I came hurtling around a bend and made mention in my commentary of the newly laid road surface and the amount of excess loose gravel on it.

Doug, at this point, had reclined his seat position to relax and was saying to Philip, 'Now, Philip, if you sit back and close your eyes, you feel like you are floating along in mid-air.'

No sooner had he made that statement, when – BANG!! – I skidded on the loose gravel, lost control and promptly hit the boundary wall.

Not exactly the way Doug wanted to be woken up and certainly not the fine example he had planned for Philip either!

Morris's News

...

During a trial in the High Court, the judge asked the accused if he had anything to say before he passed sentence.

The accused replied, 'As God is my judge, I'm innocent.'

The judge said, 'He isn't! I am! You aren't! Six months!'

A man walked into a doctor's surgery and asked the receptionist to see the doctor.

'Are you registered here?' she asked.

'I'm not sure!' replied the man. 'But I used to be!'

'When was the last time you saw the doctor, then?' she asked.

'Exactly fifteen years ago!' he replied.

'Fifteen years ago? Where have you been?' she enquired.

To which he replied, 'Peterhead Prison!!'

During the television reality show *I'm a Celebrity, Get Me Out of Here!* Peter Andre crept into Jordan's sleeping bag and nestled up close behind her.

'Is that Johnny Rotten?' enquired Jordan.

Peter replied, 'I bloody hope not, it's the only one I have!'

Police attended a call to an elderly spinster's home, after she reported an intruder in her bedroom had sexually abused her.

'How did he get in?' asked one of the police officers.

'Easy!' she replied. 'I keep a wee jar of Vaseline by the side o' my bed!'

Harry the Polis, News at Ten, somewhere in Glesca!

The Birthday Cake

• • •

One particular nightshift, whilst working alongside big Joe, I was telling him it was my son Scott's birthday the following day and that I wanted to go to a local twenty-four-hour baker's to get him a birthday cake.

Later that morning we called at the baker's and I informed one of the staff what I was looking for. Unfortunately, he said there were none left and the ones they did have were ordered beforehand. However, if I came back later, he would see what he could do for me.

On returning several hours later, the baker produced a cake for me bearing the message 'Happy Birthday, Margaret'.

'I can scrape off the name Margaret for you and put the name of your son, with a model car or something similar over the area where her name was!' said the baker.

'That's brilliant!' I responded. 'That will be perfect!'

Big Joe then asked the baker, 'By the way, who is Margaret and what about her cake?'

'They usually have two or three spare cakes in the shop, so the staff will just pipe her name in cream on to another one for her, although it won't be as fancy as this one,' he replied.

The baker then went off to take 'Margaret' off the cake and returned moments later with it all boxed up for me.

As we made our way out to the CID car, big Joe said, 'So if you have Margaret's cake, what about Margaret?'

'What *about* Margaret?' I said, totally unconcerned. 'She can just have one of the spare cakes out the shop.'

We finished our shift and went our separate ways to enjoy our days off.

As for Scott, he was delighted with his birthday party, and particularly his fancy decorated cake!

After my days off, I resumed duties with big Joe.

We were going in for our refreshment break and Joe had been muttering on about how that woman Margaret's birthday party went without a cake.

So when he went to his car to get his sandwich box, I went into the canteen, where another colleague, Eddie McIvor, was sitting having his meal.

Quickly, before big Joe came into the room, I briefed Eddie all about the birthday cake and we planned how to wind up big Joe.

We settled down and were eating our food when big Joe came in the room and sat down beside us.

I began the wind-up by asking Eddie, 'So how was your weekend, Eddie? What did you get up to?'

'Oh, the wife and I were at an old friend's surprise birthday party down at the institute!' he replied convincingly. 'It was packed with all her relatives, old friends and neighbours.'

'I take it that she had a good night, then?' I asked him.

'Absolutely superb,' he replied. 'She had emigrated twenty years ago to Canada and only came back this week to visit some friends and family, so we all got together and organised a surprise party for her, knowing it was her birthday and she might not be back here again. What a brilliant night it was!'

'Sounds like it was a lot of fun!' I said.

All the time, big Joe sat munching away on his food, totally oblivious. So I gave Eddie a nod to continue.

'Mind you! It would have been even better if that baker in the main street hadn't let us down with her surprise birthday cake,' remarked Eddie.

Big Joe's ears pricked up at this and he looked over.

'How come? What happened with her birthday cake?' big Joe enquired.

'Oh! They tried to make out that the cake was never delivered from the factory, so we didn't have one for her. The lying bastards – they probably forgot to bake it!' Eddie replied.

Now I was acting like nothing had happened and not paying too much attention to the conversation. However, Joe was kicking me under the table and pulling faces at me.

He then asked Eddie, 'So what was her name, then?'

'Who, the birthday girl? Margaret, Margaret Brown! Why, do you know her?' said Eddie convincingly.

Joe couldn't contain himself. 'Margaret?' he said, as he started sniggering and laughing nervously, spraying some of the contents of the food in his mouth, all over the table in front of him, while trying to attract my attention with the utmost subtlety. Not!

As for me, I was playing it cool, taking absolutely no notice at all and pretending to read a newspaper.

'Did you hear that, Harry?' asked Joe. 'Her birthday cake went missing and was never delivered to the shop.' He continued to laugh nervously.

Without looking up from my paper, I replied, 'And what do you want me to do about it? Call Delia Smith? By the way, I don't think it's that funny, Joe! How would you like to turn up at a surprise birthday party being held in your honour and they don't even have a cake for you?! Ye're a bit sick if you think that's remotely funny!'

Eventually Joe couldn't contain his nervous sniggering any longer and had to leave the canteen, the tears in his eyes beginning to blind him, laughing and choking on his food.

After he left, Eddie and I had a right good chuckle at his expense and at how well the wind-up had gone.

However, it didn't finish there.

When I went to the car to join Joe and resume our duty, he said, 'What do you make of that, then? That was Margaret's birthday cake you took for yer boy! How rotten can you get?'

'What are you on about?' I said.

'Eddie's old neighbour – it was her cake you took,' he replied.

I shook my head. 'Don't be stupid, Joe. It was only a wind-up!'

'Was it fuck! Ye cannae kid me. He was serious about that birthday cake. He knew all about it!' replied a convinced Joe.

'Naw!' I said, shaking my head. 'We were winding you up. I set it up with Eddie before you came into the canteen!'

'I doubt it very much, Harry. I'm not that gullible. He knew too much about it and he was even at her party!' he responded seriously.

'Of course he knew about it, but it was because I told him what to say. We set you up, ya big diddy!' I repeated.

'Naw, naw, naw! He wasn't kidding there, he was genuine. Crikey! He even said it himself – he was at the party with his wife! I suppose his wife is lying too?' replied Joe, still totally convinced a party had taken place involving this woman called Margaret.

'There wasn't any birthday party – it was a joke. I made it all up with Eddie to fool you,' I reiterated.

However, try as I might, I couldn't convince big Joe it was a set-up, or maybe he just didn't want to admit he was that stupid and was duped so easily!

On another occasion, while we were working together, I asked big Joe, 'Do you know where the saying, "What's up, Doc?" comes from?'

'Yeah, I do!' he replied. 'Bugs Bunny, of course!'

'Wrong!' I said. 'It comes from a film called *Gunfight at the OK Corral*, where Wyatt Earp and his brothers have a shootout with the Clanton family. Ward Bond played the part of Virgil Earp and Victor Mature played Doc Holliday, who was suffering from tuberculosis and was coughing up blood into his handkerchief. As he did so, Ward Bond looked over toward him and asked, "What's up, Doc?"'

He looked at me for a moment then said, 'Is that right?'

'Of course it is,' I answered, totally convincingly. 'I won a pub quiz with that answer.'

Later that evening, as I entered the front office, the station assistant immediately confronted me, 'Here, Harry, do you know where the saying, "What's up, Doc?" comes from?'

'Aye – me!' I promptly replied. 'I was winding big Joe up and told him it was Doc Holliday and he believed me and told you. Am I right?'

'Yer right,' he replied. 'He told me he had read it some-where!'

Not only was Joe gullible, but the big diddy was also a big liar!

Gynaecologists

• • •

It was a regular occurrence when I went to a party for someone to ask, 'And what do you work at?'

As soon as you mentioned the police, they would respond by saying loudly, 'Watch what ye're saying, everybody, there's a polis amongst us!'

This remark would ruin the rest of my night at the party.

It was also most notable, if you were a joiner or a plumber, they never said anything like, 'Hold on to your hinges, girls, he'll try and screw you down – he's a joiner!' or, 'Watch this wan here, girls. He's a plumber and he's likely to pull his plunger out to try and unblock yer pipes!'

So I decided that at all parties, if asked, 'What do you work at?' I was going to say, 'I'm a doctor,' but not just any old GP – I was going to be a gynaecologist!

It was amazing, after a few drinks, the number of women with a problem downstairs who wanted to discuss it in private with me upstairs and hear my professional expert advice!

Beats being a polis any time!

Yer Other Right Foot

. . .

Whilst on my motorcycle standard course, my instructor was an old, grumpy, pipe-smoking guy called Jimmy Lynch.

Now let me say immediately that he was a smashing bloke, but he had obviously taught one too many novice motorcyclists and the strain and stress of it all was beginning to show.

As was his short fuse!

One day, things weren't going well between us and Jimmy repeated several times for me to put my right foot down when stopping, in order to maintain balance and hold up the motorcycle.

In addition, radio communication between us was breaking up and I couldn't hear what direction (if any) Jimmy was giving me, although I can guess exactly what he wanted to say!

The final straw for Jimmy came when he was broadcasting to me the direction he wanted me to take and I wasn't hearing him. Well, I *was*, but I was so fed up with his shouting and swearing that I'd decided to rubber-ear him.

Suddenly an irate Jimmy overtook me and pulled in further along the road and signalled me to come alongside him.

As I pulled up alongside, I put my right leg down.

However, due to the camber of the road, the bike fell over to the left, resting on Jimmy and his bike, who quickly, while trying to hold me and my bike, blurted out,

'Yer other bloody right foot!' before he lost his own footing and the balance of his motorcycle, resulting in us both toppling over and sprawling on to the footpath in a heap.

Not exactly the dignified stop Jimmy had intended for himself.

Naughty Neighbours
· · ·

Several years ago, having bought a new house and moved to a better area, my partner and I decided to have a house-warming party and invited friends and neighbours to it.

The party went well on the night and a few new neighbours had taken up our invitation to come. However, it wasn't to turn out a late night and the majority of guests had left and gone home by eleven.

The few couples that remained were sitting in the lounge, relaxing and talking amongst themselves with some background music playing.

Suddenly, there was a loud 'rat-a-tat-tat!' on my front window, which startled everyone in the room.

I went to the front door to see who it was and there, standing in his pyjamas with his balding head and waxed moustache, was my new next-door neighbour.

A bit late and slightly underdressed for the party, I thought.

'Right!' he said sternly. 'Time to finish up and switch that music off. Some of us have to go to bed now!'

Surprised and shocked at this interruption, I replied, 'Well, please don't let me stop you, sir. Off you go, then!'

'I'm talking about you as well!' he said.

'Is that right?' I responded. 'Well, don't you worry yourself about me, I'll be just fine. Now, night-night!'

I then closed the door on him.

As I returned to the lounge, I was to learn from one of my party guests that my gatecrashing next-door neighbour was a bit of an old-fashioned party-pooper who tried to rule the area.

However, over the following months he proved to be a total nightmare and would regularly knock on my window, or come to my front door, dressed like Wee Willie Winkie, if I was playing music or my dog barked.

On one particular night, my dog was barking and I opened the door and went out to see what was up. As I did, I saw my neighbour, Willie, standing in my driveway.

'You'd better quieten your dog. It's five past eleven. They're not allowed to bark after eleven!' he said with a voice of authority.

I looked at him standing in my driveway and said, 'It might be a watchdog, sir, but that doesn't mean it can tell the time! Anyway, what are you doing on my property, annoying my dog?'

'Annoying your dog?! I know what I'll do with your bloody dog!' he said. 'And I'll be writing to your chief constable!'

'Right, that's it! Get out of my driveway,' I told him. 'Come in here again without asking and I'll put my boot up yer saggy arse.'

The next evening, I was returning home late from a night out with my shift and was passing a house displaying an estate agent's 'for sale' notice in the front garden.

I couldn't resist it – I took possession of it and erected the board in the middle of my estranged neighbour's front garden.

Next morning, as I left early for my shift, I had a good laugh to myself, looking at the sign and thinking how he would react.

Later the same day, on returning home, I noticed a different estate agent's sign erected in his garden. I immediately thought this was the work of my partner but, as it turned out, it was genuine and he was moving.

However, I would like to believe, in my own way, I helped make up his mind that it was time to move on!

I think I'm due commission from the estate agents!

Funny Text

. . .

I received a text to my mobile phone from my oldest brother which read: 'The police have found an unidentified body of a male, floating in the River Clyde, next to the Govan Docks. He is described as having false teeth, shaggy beard, balding, with bags under both eyes and suffering from excessive obesity! Please text me back immediately, to confirm you're all right. Allan.'

The Glesca Fair Holidays

• • •

The Glasgow Airport

There was a large queue forming at the airport check-in as the Glesca holidaymakers arrived for their annual trek to sunny Spain, por favor!

Georgina ('call me Georgie') and William ('call me Wullie') arrived in style, alighting from a black 'hack' taxi and stumbled through the automatic sliding doors, each with a trolley stacked high with luggage.

Georgie was built like the proverbial brick shithouse with a pair of tits that could breastfeed a village community of a Third World country for an entire week and still struggle to lose any weight.

Wullie was smaller in height, fat and balding. He was also wearing a pair of yellow shorts with a red top and *Terminator* sunglasses, perched on top of his head.

The only thing missing was a red nose and big shoes.

'Shit, Georgie!' said Wullie. 'Wid ye look at that queue! I think the whole a' Glesca is goin' on holiday.'

'Jist pray they're no' gaun' where we're gaun', Wullie! We'll never get near the beach!' replied Georgie.

The Gran'weans Arrive

Several young girls appeared in the terminal building and spotted Georgie and Wullie in the check-in queue.

'Granny! Granda!' They made their way towards them, with their arms outstretched.

It was the gran'weans!

'Oh, look, Wullie! There's Lisa-Marie with the lassies tae say cheerio tae us,' Georgie called out to them. 'Chelsea! Kylie! Demi! Get o'er here and gie yer granny a big kiss and a cuddle.'

As they all gathered around Georgie, cuddling her, she asked, 'Where's wee Bethney and Victoria?'

'My da's baby-sitting them two. Victoria's got a rash oan her bum and Bethney's teething and widnae stop greetin'!' replied Demi.

Wullie asked Lisa-Marie, 'How much is this going tae cost us?'

'Aw, stop it, Da! The weans jist wanted tae say "au revoir" tae ye both afore ye go. Ah mean, it's yer first holiday abroad efter aw,' replied Lisa-Marie.

'Well, I just hope yer brothers and sisters are no' gonnae make a personal appearance wi' *their* weans, 'cause there's nae mer room in the airport,' he said sincerely.

'Ye *wid* have a big family, Da,' said Lisa-Marie.

'Nae telly, hen. I'm having tae watch aw the auld repeats o' *Perry Mason* and *Columbo* tae try an' catch up wi' the TV programmes I missed 'cause o' you lot!' he replied.

As they got closer to the check-in desk, another young family appeared and were instantly recognised. It was their son with four of his kids.

'Mammy, look!' called Lisa-Marie. 'There's oor Dominic wi' Wulliam and the boys!'

As they approached Georgie, Wulliam called out, 'Whit's this, Maw? Trying tae dae a moonlight fae the hoose without crackin' a light tae yer weans?'

'Aye! She's eloping wi' ma granda fur a dirty week abroad,' said Chelsea.

'Nae chance! Yer Granda and I don't dae that any more!' said Georgie, before turning to one of her grandsons.

'Ho, Brooklyn son, gie yer granny a big hug!' she said.

As Brooklyn embraced Georgie, he informed her, 'The triplets are here as well, Granny!'

'Where ur they?' she asked with excitement.

At that, his three other brothers appeared. She threw her arms out to greet them as she shouted, 'John-Paul, Georgie and Ringo, o'er here!' She then turned to Wullie and said, 'I don't believe it!'

'Neither does the airport security!' remarked Wullie. 'One thing's fur sure – there's nae chance o' it getting bombed 'cause there's nae room fur anybody else in the airport.'

The Airport Check-In

A voice called out in the check-in hall.

'Wullie! Wullie Hill! I thought it wis you. Where ur ye flying aff tae?'

Wullie looked over and recognised the caller immediately.

'Oh, hallo there, Danny!' he replied.

'Me and Georgie are aff tae Magaluf fur a wee holiday. A sort o' second honeymoon. Mind you, we never had a first wan, wi' her pregnant wi' oor Wulliam. Whit aboot yersel'?' asked Wullie.

'The very same! "Shagaluf", here we come! The burd got some extra dosh fae the social – wan o' them crisis loans – so we managed to get booked up for the sun. We were originally goin' tae that "Fucket"!'

Lisa-Marie interrupted him, 'Ah think ye mean Phuket.'

' "Fooky", "Fucket", it's the same thing, hen," responded Danny. 'Anyway, my burd didnae like the idea o' aw them ladyboys hangin' aboot us. I think she wis a bit jealous they might make a play for me.' He then paused and pointed over to her. 'There she's there in the queue, minding aw the gear!' he added.

Wullie and Lisa-Marie looked over towards her.

'I thought ye couldnae fly if ye were heavily pregnant?' enquired a surprised Lisa-Marie.

'Who, her? Naw, naw! She's no' pregnant, doll, she's jist a fat greedy cow. But she's built for comfort and a raving sex-mad nympho tae boot!' Danny then nudged Wullie and added, '*You* know whit Ah mean Wullie – a bit like your Georgie?'

'Aye! Ah think I know whit ye mean, Danny,' replied Wullie.

'So whit does she see in *you*, then?' asked Lisa-Marie sarcastically.

'The perfect man, hen!' replied Danny. 'Somebody wi' a ten-inch tongue that can breathe through his ears!'

Danny looked at some of the kids surrounding them.

'Is this your lot, Wullie?' he asked.

'Aye, some o' them,' replied Wullie.

'How many weans have you got, then?' asked Danny.

'We have thirteen weans, twenty-eight gran'weans and four great-gran'weans!' replied Wullie.

'Thirteen, twenty-eight and four? Fuck me!' said a

surprised Danny. 'I hope they're no' aw goin' wi' ye oan the same flight!'

'Naw, naw! They've jist come tae say cheerio,' replied Wullie.

Danny repeated, 'Thirteen, twenty-eight and four! Crikey, Wullie, your seedlings are spreading quicker than the bird flu virus.'

There was a slight pause before Danny continued, 'If ye threw a stone up in the air in Glesca, it's liable tae come doon and hit wan o' your gran'weans! Now I know where ye got the nickname, big Wullie!'

'Aye, right!' answered Wullie, having heard it all before and slightly embarrassed with Lisa-Marie standing beside him.

'Naw, seriously, Wullie, Britain must come right oot the water when your family go on holiday together!' continued Danny.

Not getting a lot of response back from Wullie, Danny said, 'Well, I better get back tae the burd afore she misses me and starts chatting up some other hunk o' burning love in the queue.' He paused, turned back and then repeated, 'Thirteen, twenty-eight and four!' He shook his head. 'You've done some amount o' humping, wee man. Yer missus must o' been programmed like a caged battery hen. I bet ye made a fortune in family allowance.'

Wullie gave him an icy stare, as if to say 'enough!'

Danny got the message and returned to his burd in the next check-in queue.

Georgie called out, 'Right, Wullie, that's us. Ye've tae put the baggage oan the movin' track tae be labelled.' Turning to her son, she said, 'Dominic! You and Wulliam gie yer da a haun wi' the cases.' She paused, before whispering, 'And tell yer da tae memorise every bit o' luggage we put on, jist in case it gets blagged afore it reaches Spain!'

'Whit dae ye think it is, Maw? *The Generation Game*?!' said Dominic. 'Jim Davidson couldnae memorise that lot, never mind my da! It takes him aw his time to remember wur names. Anyways, the only way ye can lose it oan a flight is if yer plane gets hijacked.'

However, between them Dominic and Wulliam managed to load the luggage on to the conveyor belt.

The check-in girl called over to her colleague, 'Here's another yin, Patsy. Packed the entire hoose to go on holiday.' She then turned to Georgie. 'Did ye pack the bags yersel' love?'

Georgie replied in all sincerity, 'Well, ye've got tae, hen, 'cause nae bloody man is gonnae dae it for ye, know whit Ah mean? Everything gets crushed tae buggery wi' them.'

She called over to her colleague again, 'I might have known, Patsy. The wife packed the cases!'

The Mile-High Club

Over in the other queue, Danny and his burd, Sinitta, were next to check in. Danny was separating the luggage and asked Sinitta, 'D'you want yer holdall?'

'Definitely,' replied Sinitta enthusiastically. 'But let's wait tae we get oan the plane first and we can join the shag-me-high-up club.'

'I think ye mean the Mile High Club,' said Danny

disgustedly. 'But Ah'm no' talking aboot that, ya silly cow. I'm asking do you want yer holdall with you, as hand luggage on the plane?'

'Oh, sorry about the misunderstanding, Danny,' she replied.

With all the passengers aboard, the aeroplane sped along the runway and was airborne, prior to reaching the Erskine Bridge Toll.

The Outward Flight

Within ten minutes of taking off, Georgie had a flask of hot water and cuppa soups out and was also making up sandwiches from her bag, brimming with a plain loaf of bread, pork pies, salad tomatoes, iceberg lettuce, roast chicken and ham.

As the flight hostess approached, Georgie beckoned her over.

'Listen, hen, d'you want a wee hot cuppa soups and a ham or chicken salad sandwich afore ye start yer shift? I'm jist making them up fresh.'

'Er, no, thank you, but it was nice of you to ask,' replied a rather bemused hostess.

'Well, mind and ask the pilot and his mates if they'd aw like wan for their tea break!' said Georgie. 'We've plenty tae eat wi' us. I can even gie ye a slice o' juicy melon!'

'Oh, right, well, if you could just try and keep it out of sight from Wilma, the head stewardess, because it's not really allowed on the plane!' the hostess informed her.

'Howzat?' asked Georgie. 'Have ye got a canteen?'

'Well, no, but we actually come round selling food and drinks on the plane to you!' explained the flight hostess.

'Aw right! Sorry, hen, you can dae without competition frae me when you're trying tae make a few bob for yersel'! Anyhow, dinnae you worry, pet. I'll keep shtum aboot my sandwiches!' replied Georgie in all innocence, then added, 'Mind and gie me a shout if ye run out o' yours and I'll make ye up some o' mine tae sell!'

'Thanks for the offer,' replied the hostess before walking off completely bemused.

Later on, as the hostess was collecting the airline magazines, Georgie said to her, 'I've got a few pies and a chicken drum-stick left if you would like them for yer return flight back to Glesca.'

'That's very kind of you, but we'll be restocking with food when we land in Spain!' replied the hostess.

Touchdown in Magaluf, Spain

The plane eventually touched down and Georgie headed off to the toilets inside the airport terminal while Wullie met up with Danny and Sinitta in the baggage collection hall.

'Ho, Wullie! I nearly keecht my Y-fronts when we hit that patch o' turbulence. Whit wis that all aboot?' asked Danny.

'Turbulence?' replied a surprised Wullie. 'Is that whit it wis? I better apologise tae oor Georgie when she comes oot the bog! I actually thought it wis her farting like a four-bob rocket efter eating aw they pork pies 'n' beans during the flight. Mind you, now that you mention it, I never smelt anything!'

'I thought we were a bit low when he flew o'er that car boot sale!' added Sinitta. 'I thought for a minute the pilot had a stall.'

'Low?! I could see the prices oan some o' the stalls!' said Wullie. 'I even thought at one point we were goin' tae pass through the toll on the Erskine Bridge!'

'Well, when you travel with JCB Cheap Flight Airlines, you dig yer own grave!' remarked Danny.

At that, Georgie returned and they collected their luggage before going outside the terminal building to hire a taxi.

'Let me dae the talking, Wullie!' said Georgie.

'Why would I want tae change the habit o' a lifetime, hen?' replied Wullie facetiously.

'Well, ye know whit Ah mean, Wullie! Efter aw, I watched every episode o' that BBC Spanish soap *Eldorado* so I think I've picked up a few words o' the lingo. You've just got tae add an "o" on the end o' everything ye say.'

She approached the first taxi driver. 'Excuso meo, por favor! Dos uno speako di Español?'

The taxi driver looked at her and answered, 'Sí, señora, I do, I am Spanish!'

'Oh, goodo!' replied Georgie. 'How mucho denero to drive us to oor apartmento in Magalufo?'

'How many people?' enquired the driver in perfect English.

'Justo the dos of uso and our baggios,' said Georgie, totally oblivious of the driver's perfect response in English.

'Veinte euros!' replied the driver. 'Sorry – twenty euros!'

'Righto!' said Georgie immediately. 'You are hiredo, por favor.'

All the while, Wullie was standing in awe of Georgie and amazed by her total command of a foreign tongue and ability to converse with the taxi driver.

They were then conveyed to their accommodation.

Completely shattered from the flight, they both fell into bed for a good night's sleep.

The Apartment Accommodation

Next morning, Wullie was roused by the smell of bacon and eggs being cooked by Georgie.

'Aw, darling! Did you get up early and go shopping?' asked Wullie.

'Dinnae be daft. I brought it wi' us! Just in case they didnae sell oor kind o' grub oot here,' replied Georgie.

Wullie approached her. 'Can I help ye wi' anything?' he asked.

'Aye, ye can put the kettle oan and make us a brew,' replied Georgie. 'I'm thirsting fur a Nambarrie.'

As Wullie filled the kettle, he looked about the kitchen area.

'Here! That toaster looks like oors!'

'It *is* oors!' said Georgie with a straight face. 'And the kettle, frying pan, egg poacher, coffee mugs and aw the cutlery! I didnae want tae take the chance o' there no' being any stuff in the flat and bein' left wi' nuthin' tae cook with!'

Wullie continued to look around.

'Please tell me that's no' oor bloody cooker yer using?' he asked Georgie sarcastically.

'Don't be ridiculous, Wullie! I couldnae possibly pack a bloody cooker!' Then under her breath she said, 'But the George Foreman grill and the Breville toastie are both oors.'

Night Out on the Town

Later that week, fed up with Georgie's fry-up morning, noon and night, Wullie suggested they hit the town and sample some of the local Spanish cuisine for a change.

'As long as it's no' they wee Spanish Tampax dishes,' said Georgie. 'I'm starving.'

They entered a Spanish restaurant and were approached by the waiter, who asked, 'Quesiera una mesa cerca la ventana para dos?'

Wullie hadn't a clue what the waiter had just asked and looked at Georgie for some guidance.

Georgie paused for a 'momento', then said, 'Ventana? Naw! It's notto ours. We drive a Fordo Caprio at homo, por favor!'

The confused waiter then showed them to their table, 'not near to the window'.

Ordering Up a Meal

Wullie then asked the waiter to recommend a Spanish dish.

The waiter suggested the local paella! However, he

pointed out the chef's speciality dish of the night was fresh lobster.

Wullie settled for his first ever lobster dish, while Georgie chose to be adventurous and go for the fish and chips, with a cheap bottle of Spanish house plonk as a chaser!

'In fact, givvo us uno bottle ovvo "Pi-at the Door" wino, por favor!' Georgie ordered.

They sat there listening to the background music and soaking up the ambience of their surroundings, when the kitchen door opened and the waiter approached with their meals.

As the lobster was placed in front of Wullie, he quickly surveyed his dish and noticed his long-awaited first lobster only had one claw, which he immediately drew to the attention of Georgie, who took no time in calling the waiter back and enquiring in her own fluent Spanish lingo, 'Excuso meo une momento, Manuel! Uno lobstero hasso onlyo juan leggo! How commo, pray tello meo?'

'Ah, sí, señora!' replied the waiter. 'El langosta es combate con el otra langosta y perdido una pinza!'

Wullie and Georgie both looked at him for a moment with a blank expression on their faces, then Wullie said to Georgie, 'Well, you're bifocal, hen, tell us, whit did he say?'

Before Georgie could speak, the waiter turned to her and replied in perfect English, 'I say to you that your lobster was involved in a fight with another lobster in the tank and lost one of his claws.'

'Lost his claw in a fight, did he?' said Wullie, pausing for a moment before continuing, 'Well! Any chance ye could take it back tae the kitchen and bring me the winner?!'

Meeting Up With the Friends

Later that same week, before they were due to fly back home, they met up with other friends from Glesca.

Wullie had his shirt unbuttoned to the waist and was proudly displaying a large crucifix round his neck.

'How's it gaun, Wullie?' asked Sam. 'I didnae know ye were a medallion man. It's hard to tell if you're wearing that crucifix or affixed to it!'

'Aye, well! It wis a wee pressie frae Georgie,' explained Wullie. 'She bought it frae wan o' the "lookie-lookie" men. He had loads o' good gear wi' him. Fishing rods, watches, sunglasses, and it wis really cheap as well. By the way, he swore it wis genuine gold-plated, none o' yer fake shit.'

'You jist swore as well, but that disnae make whit ye're saying genuine!' replied Sam.

As they sat down at a table outside the pub to enjoy a cool beer, Sam asked Wullie, 'Whit aboot wee Jackie Wilson then?'

'Wee Jackie Wilson? Whit aboot him?' enquired Wullie.

'He's flipped! Lost his marbles!' replied Sam. The polis found him wanderin' aboot the street in his pyjamas. They say he's been showing signs o' losing it for a while noo.'

'Whit happened to him?' asked Wullie.

'Well, they've put him away in wan o' them nursing homes for an assessment,' said Sam.

'Who wid have thought that o' him, then?' remarked Wullie, pausing for a moment while considering what he has just heard. 'Wee Jackie Wilson, the bookies' runner?' he said as he shook his head.

'Aye, wee Jackie Wilson!' repeated Sam. 'Apparently the staff have nicknamed him "Jack the Clipper", 'cause they caught him wan night wandering aboot the ward wi' a pair o' nail clippers. He wis going round the ither patients in the ward, lifting up their bed sheets and cutting their toenails while they were sleeping!'

Wullie laughed at the thought of it and said, 'Maybe he was a chiropodist in another life!'

'Well, he must have been a dog as well, 'cause seemingly he bit another patient and was caught wi' the nurse, lifting his leg and pissing on some o' their hospital beds.'

'Ye'd think a man o' his age wid be housetrained!' joked Wullie.

Sam continued with more gossip: 'Anyways, afore I left, I heard he managed tae get haud o' a razor and shaved two patients and gave another auld yin a Yul Brynner! Her family were fizzing when they arrived at visiting time to discover their wee mammy sitting there like Sinead O'Connor wi' her heid aw shaved.'

Passing the Time Together

While the two of them were passing the time talking about mutual friends, Danny was passing by with Sinitta and spotted them.

'Check this out, Sinitta! It's Victor and Jack from *Still Game*.'

Danny then looked at the two of them sitting there and continued, 'Eyeing up all the young burds, are we, boys?'

'Not at all, Danny! Definitely not!' they replied in unison.

'Well, if ye are, ye'd be better aff doon at the beach bar. It's surrounded wi' big bare diddies hanging aboot it and I'm no' jist talking aboot the big blond German musclemen either!' said Danny.

'This is good enough for me,' said Sam. 'It's like a scene from *Goldfinger* . . . Pussy Galore!'

'Have ye's had a good time then, you two?' enquired Wullie.

'We've had a smashing time,' replied Sinitta. 'And whit a difference it made having yer ain wee lavvy at the bottom o' yer bed!'

'It's called an "end-suite" room,' remarked Sam.

'Whitever!' said Danny. 'It was ideal for us, 'cause Sin's no' exactly a pretty sight during the night when she's bursting for a single fish and the last thing ye want is tae bump intae her in the corridor!'

The Men Talk

Sinitta then went inside the pub to meet up with Georgie and Sam's wife Ella.

'Whit's up wi' yer burd's lips, Danny?' enquired Wullie.

'Herpes!' replied Danny, dismissive of it. 'She gets it aw

the time wi' lying oot in the sun. So she says! And whit's yer hotel like, Sam?'

'The hotel is aw right, but trying tae get a haud o' the courier is a nightmare,' said Sam. 'All she ever says is, "Two minutes", "I'll be with you in two minutes", "Just give me two minutes". Two minutes? Whit she really means is two fuckin' days! I've jist gave up on her!'

As the men sat there drinking, Sam was staring at the three partners seated inside the bar and remarked, 'See your burd, Danny, I'm jist watching her. She cannae half talk! She's like a gattling gub!'

'True, Sam! But you'll notice she has a slight impediment! She has to pause noo and again to breathe!' replied Danny.

There was a lull as all three men looked over at their partners, before Sam continued, 'See my Ella? She reminds me o' a white dove – she's right into peace and love, and likes tae "coo, coo, coory" in!'

'Well, since ye've mentioned it,' said Wullie, 'see my Georgie? She reminds me o' a robin – she's got a lovely pair o' big breasts, voluptuous big red breasts!'

'Whit aboot your Sinitta, Danny? Whit fine feathered burd describes her attributes best?' enquired Sam.

'Her?' replied Danny, pausing for a moment, giving it considerable thought. 'Probably a thrush!'

'A thrush? So is she a good singer, then?' asked Sam.

'Naw,' responded Danny. 'She's jist an irritating bitch!'

Girlie Talk at the Bar

Meanwhile, inside the pub with the girls, Sinitta was asking, 'How are ye, Georgie? Are ye enjoying yerself?'

'Bloody marvellous, hen! I'm really having a ball here!' replied Georgie before asking, 'And whit aboot you, hen? I can see ye're walking kind o' funny. Did ye get badly sunburnt?'

'Naw!' replied Sinitta. At that she took Georgie's arm and led her over towards the bar. 'Come o'er tae the bar for a drink tae Ah tell ye whit happened.' She turned back to the table and said, 'You as well, Ella!'

They all took seats around the bar and Georgie ordered the drinks for them.

'Excuso, Manuel, couldo youo getto dos Bacardio and Coka, endo uno bloody Maryo, por favor?'

'Ye're like a native talking there, Georgie. Ye've fairly picked up the lingo!' remarked Sinitta. 'Ye'd pass for a local!'

'I owe it all tae that *Eldorado*,' replied Georgie, pleased with herself.

'Whit, the wine?' asked Sinitta.

'Naw! The soap, ya silly cow!' responded Georgie.

At that, the young barman answered in a broad Geordie accent, 'Nae problem, lass, that's two Bacardis with Coke and a Bloody Mary. Just tak a seat at a table and I'll bring you them o'er, like!'

The women returned to the table and Sinitta asked, 'Huv any o' ye been in that Señora Annie Summers sex shop along the road?'

'Oh, naw, Ah couldnae!' replied Georgie. 'My weans wid call me for everything if they knew I went in there.' She paused for a moment before continuing, 'But you're much younger and can get away wi' it, Sinitta!'

'Aye, well, maybe so, but I'm not embarrassed to say, "Sticks and stones will break my bones, but whips and chains excite me!" And Danny, of course. Mind you, he's that bloody horny, a watch chain excites him! So I went in and got a pair o' they sexy G-strings and wore them for Danny. Uncomfortable or whit?!'

'Anyways, he thinks they'll lead him tae ma G spot. A miner's helmet and a map of the female body couldnae lead him tae it. Three days later, the bloody things are cutting into me and I'm red raw doon below. Mind you, I got waxed last week and they gave me a proper Brazilian afore I left Scotland, but I think they gave me Ronaldhino and left in his big buck teeth, because something is jagging me and it's stinging like buggery doon there, especially wi' me sweating so much.

So, I've whipped them aff and went straight back tae the shop wi' them and complained. Does it no' turn oot I've been wearing the bloody things back tae front and the thin strip goes between the cheeks o' yer erse! They've refused tae change them because they had been worn but, fortunately, they wurnae as dear as I told Danny, so I'll gie ye them, Georgie, as a present for wan o' yer daughters!'

Georgie gave her a look, as if to say, 'Don't think so, Sinitta!'

'By the way,' continued Sinitta, 'that randy bugger

Danny said tae me, "Get yersel' a girlie vibrator while ye're in there!" So I'm looking aboot and Ah spot this white wan wi' a big red knob-end, nice shape, nuthin' too fancy, 'cause Ah hate they wans wi' aw the nobbly bits. So I thought tae mysel', that'll dae for me. I called to the assistant, who just happened to look like Ricky Martin – I could have sucked the make-up aff him there and then – Here, pal!" Ah shouted. "Any chance ye could gie me that big red and white vibrator behind you?" He turned around and looked at it for a moment then replied, "I cannot give you that one, señorita, that is what you call my coffee flask!"'

The Last Supper

Later, the three couples agreed to meet up for a last-night meal and during the evening, Danny looked across the table at Sinitta, who was dressed up in more coloured feathers than a tropical parrot, with a huge purple and red nookie badge prominent on the side of her neck, and announced for all to hear, 'I cannae wait till we get back tae the hotel room so I can rip yer knickers aff, Sinitta!'

Georgie, Wullie, Sam 'n' Ella looked at each other and raised their eyebrows at this very loud and personal outburst.

Then Danny added, ''Cause they've been cutting into my bloody leg aw night!'

At that, Danny and Sinitta burst out laughing, followed by the others, who saw the funny side.

While perusing the menu, Danny said, 'Huv ye noticed ye cannae get a decent Chic Murray here?'

'That's cause ye're in Spain, ya plonker, and no' India!' said Sam.

'Whit is "man get out"?' Sinitta asked Ella.

'Where does it say that?'

'Number thirty-four on the menu – "Lamb on the bone, roast potatoes and man get out" – see it?'

'That's "mangetout", ya silly cow! It's like a flat green bean,' replied Ella.

At the end of the night, Wullie commented, 'Jist as well the Spanish food and hygiene didnae come in here tonight! The restaurant might have been shut down when they found Sam 'n' Ella present!'

'Heard it afore, Wullie!' said a disgruntled Sam, shaking his head.

'OK, then, Georgie, dae yer stuff and ask the waiter tae bring us the bill!' said Wullie.

Danny, slightly worse off with the amount of alcohol he had consumed, remarked, 'Better still, Georgie, ask him tae dae an impression o' a pelican and stick his bill up his arse!'

Georgie summoned the waiter to the table, with the use of some clever sign language. 'Ho! Camerero! El billo! Por favor.'

'Let Sinitta ask him,' said Danny. 'She's got her A-level in languages!' Turning to Sinitta, he said, 'Go for it, Sin!'

Sinitta was reluctant, but Danny was very persuasive. 'Go on!'

The waiter was standing patiently, waiting to hear what it was they would like to order next.

Sinitta began, 'Eh . . . je suis la porte, ouvrez la fenêtre, por favor!'

The waiter stared at her for a moment and then said, 'Perdone, señora?'

He then bent down and whispered to her, 'Excuse me, señora, but I believe you have just spoken to me in French and said, "I am the door, open the window, please"!'

Sinitta looked at him, slightly flustered, then turned to Georgie and said, 'You better ask him, Georgie, he obviously doesn't understand my "Michael Thomas" higher Spanish. It's maybe my Glesca accent!'

Georgie took over and said, 'Excuso, Manuel! Canno youo bringo une billo, por favor?'

'Yes, señora, I can bring you the bill,' replied the waiter.

'There ye go, nae problemo!' remarked a proud Wullie.

While awaiting the bill, Georgie asked them all, 'Does anybody fancy a fruit yogurt or a Blue Riband biscuit? I've got a few left in my bag.'

However, nobody took up Georgie's offer.

The three couples parted company and returned to their respective accommodation to pack for the morning flight back home to Bonnie Scotland.

The Return Flight Home

Next morning was a sight to behold as Georgie and Wullie arrived at the airport carrying five large, colourful Spanish donkeys and wearing eight Mexican-style sombreros between them.

Oh, and two rugs draped over their shoulders, from the 'lookie, lookie' man.

As they approached, Danny and Sinitta were already at the check-in.

Danny was staring at Wullie carrying all the Spanish gifts, so Wullie remarked, 'A wee something for the gran'weans. Ye know how it is.'

'Crikey, Wullie, ye came bursting through they doors there like Don Quixote! I had tae look twice,' said Danny. 'Tell me this – did ye get a taxi tae the airport, or did you and Georgie jist ride o'er here on wan o' yer herd o' donkeys?'

Arriving Back In Glasgow

Finally, after a good laugh and what seemed like a short week, Wullie and Georgie landed back at Glesca airport, where there wasn't a shortage of family members swelling the crowds in the arrivals hall, waiting to greet them.

'Wullie!' Danny shouted over. 'There's a bigger crowd waiting for you at the airport than there was for the Beatles!'

As he bent down and picked up his last piece of luggage from the conveyor belt, he was about to leave the airport building but couldn't resist one last call to Wullie.

'Here, wee man. I think wan o' yer donkeys jist shat in the baggage hall!'

Wullie smiled back and simply replied, 'Hasta la vista, Danny-o! Or, as we say in Glesca . . . gerrit up ye, ya fanny!'

My Appreciation

. . .

The author would like to thank you for buying this book and hopes that you had as much fun reading it, as he had writing and compiling it.

The author would also like to thank the many police colleagues/characters who made it possible to write about all this but impossible to tell the real truth.

The author would also like to add that most of the names have been changed to protect the guilty and most of the stories have been exaggerated!

The Harry the Polis cartoons were created and written by Harry Morris and illustrated by Derek Seal.

Harry Morris, who appears courtesy of his parents, is available as an after dinner speaker for functions and can be contacted by email at:

harry.morris51@virgin.net

Or by post:

PO BOX 7031, GLASGOW, G44 3YN. SCOTLAND.